In Realms Beyond

Book One of the Peter Chronicles

AL MINER and LAMA SING

CoCreations Publishing

In Realms Beyond: Book One of the Peter Chronicles
Copyright ©1990 by Al Miner

Cover art and book design by Susan M. Miner

ISBN -13   978-0-9791262-3-9
ISBN -10   0-9791262-3-1

1. Lama Sing 2. Psychics 3. Trance Channels 4. Life After Death
5. The Peter Project
I. Miner, Al II. Lama Sing III. Title

Library of Congress Control Number: 2007902144

Printed in the United States of America

For books and products, or to write Al Miner,
visit our website: **www.lamasing.net**

Dedication

To Lama Sing, for more than thirty years of loving service to the world. Without you, the story of a man we call Peter would never have been told.

With gratitude to my dear friends who encouraged the continuation of the "Peter readings," and who remain unwavering in their enthusiasm to this day.

And to Susan, whose love, inspiration, and tireless dedication brought this book into reality.

Contents

About Lama Sing

More than thirty years ago for our convenience, the one through whom this information flows accepted the name Lama Sing, though it was stated they, themselves, have no need for names or titles.

"We identify ourselves only as servants of God, dedicated to you, our brothers and sisters in the Earth."

℘

"The source, which has become known as Lama Sing is, indeed, a teacher to the Channel. The Channel has functioned with this source in previous life experiences not limited to the Earth or physical planes. The source, known as Lama Sing, is a part of the Channel's group soul purpose, which then functions under a different accord or tenet, celestially speaking.

"Do not associate the title "Lama Sing" as an individual name. Though the name has been an individual soul's name in past, it should not be thought of just as an individual in its present use or connotation but, rather, as a group or purpose, rather than a name. It would be as though one were speaking to a consciousness, which is comprised of collective aspects. We humbly pray this is of some clarity to you."

–Lama Sing

About These Works

"Know that it is our prayer throughout eternity that these works shall heighten that consciousness in each who shall hear it, and only to the need and the usefulness of thy soul's will do we ask that it be given. Each shall hear differently, for each is the unique creation of God—each one hears within himself or herself, and shall understand a different word, a different comprehension. So, dwell not upon this word or that, but cleave unto the spirit, which is given in each."

℘

"The purposes of functioning through this Channel are to give to mankind only that as would urge them to find God within themselves. There is no wish among those present here that these words shall ring throughout eternity or be inscribed in great books or great halls. It would rather be our most humble prayer that the thoughts which are given with these words should have some meaning in the hearts and minds of those who hear them; and that the thoughts and attitudes shall live on, not these words or these works or the name surrounding same."

-Lama Sing

About This Channel

"Channel is that term given generally to those who enable themselves to be, as much as possible, open and passable in terms of information that can pass through them from the Universal Consciousness, or other such which are not associated in the direct sense with their finite consciousness of the current incarnation."

ℭℨ

"This Channel shall not always be with thee in the Earth. There will be that time wherein the Father shall call him again unto these realms. See? Then what shall there be in his stead?

"Shall there be a temple unto him as an individual? It would be our prayer that this shall not be so. If thee would regard him, everyone, as a brother, then this is a source of joy. But do not edify nor build temples, for there is but one God.

"It is the purpose of this Channel to be a lamp unto your footsteps, to be your servant, and to be that which gives unto you when you are needy and which shares with you when you are joyous. But we, here, and the Channel, are no greater than the least of thee."

-Lama Sing

Foreword

In 1976 I was living in Virginia Beach, Virginia, when Hugh Lynn Cayce, Edgar Cayce's son, told me that a new young and exciting psychic was coming to town and that I should have a reading from him. At the time I was giving introductory talks about Edgar Cayce at the Association for Research and Enlightenment, which provides access to Edgar Cayce's 14,000 readings. In many of those readings Edgar Cayce said, "You are your own psychic, you can do what I do." Being so steeped in that mindset, naturally I said, "No, thank you. I am very intuitive."

Hugh Lynn was very persistent: "Sandra this young man is the best psychic I've heard since my Dad died and you know how long ago that was 1945, this is 1976." I said okay.

Al Miner was staying at the Hilton Hotel on the beach, and when I arrived for my reading he was already in a deep state of relaxation. The wind was billowing the curtains and Al was laid out on the bed. With a washcloth over his eyes and a big microphone hanging over his mouth, he looked pretty scary to me. I almost left, but remembering Hugh Lynn's words, thought better of it and sat down as his wife conducted the session.

As she began praying, the air in the room seemed to become liquid, permeable, smooth against my face. A penetrating quality of love and acceptance washed over me. I knew that this wasn't possible, yet my every emotional, mental, and physical sense was telling me that I was completely and totally loved. Tears streamed down my face as wave after wave of this intense love filled me.

Then Al began to channel Lama Sing. This reading was the turning point of my life. I was recently divorced, had two small children, and was eager as well as apprehensive to make a new start. Lama Sing, through Al, gave me such insight into who I was and what I was meant to do that, in a sense, the 27 year old that I was then, saw my past, present, and future from a perspective that has informed my life every day since.

I think this book has the potential to transform the lives of its readers in much the same way.

Sandra Martin
ParaView Productions

It Begins

He dims the lights in his office, turns off the phone, and slips into the recliner beside the rack of recording equipment. Reaching over, he sorts through the music to find a piece he feels will appeal to him and perhaps fit the topic for this reading, and then starts the player and the recording.

As though reaching out to embrace him, the music is now playing softly in the background. The footrest pops up as he leans back in the recliner. Looking rather like an old dog pawing at his blanket, arranging it to prevent any discomfort from disrupting his nap, he begins to fidget, positioning himself in his chair until everything feels just right.

He closes his eyes and for a few moments drifts into the encroaching darkness, checking his comfort, testing the level of his relaxation, looking for those certain symbols personal to him that indicate he is sufficiently balanced to be able to give this reading. Satisfied, he strains to return from his already shifting consciousness, and opens his eyes to switch off the music and adjust the mic hanging overhead. As he settles back into position, the darkness envelops him once again. He knows he has only moments before he is gone from the consciousness of his Earthly body, and he forces himself to utter his prayer.

"This is January 31, 1990," comes the voice of Al Miner, beginning as he has for more than twenty years and nearly 7000 readings to this point. "This reading is code #V-630. The title of the reading is 'Colors and Their Influences.' We pray of you, Father, that you would guide us to the highest and best possible information that would contribute to the greatest extent to our knowledge and our guidance in rediscovering our true nature. As always, we thank you, Father. Amen." Moments later, he is gone.

Time passes.

The breathing begins to change... deepening, slowing.

Finally, the lips begin to purse and flex, as though warming up for some strange exercise, and the silence is broken.

Using his own voice, accent and grammatical structure, Lama Sing borrows the body, this channel, to offer a prayer from the group of which Lama Sing is a part, *"Lord, we know that Thou art with us in all things, and, thus, it is our prayer that we might herein accomplish Thy will and Thy purpose. We pray further that Thou would grant us the presence of the Master, The Christ, so as to impart through His Spirit the healing grace, love, compassion, and wisdom as shall inspire within all the ability to better know themselves at one with Thee. We pray further on behalf of all those souls in all realms who, being presently in some need, have none in joyous prayer on their behalf. It is with humble joy that we thank Thee, Father, for this opportunity of service in Thy name. Amen."*

The reading begins, *"Each of you on Earth is aware of the impact of the varying colors in your realm upon the attitude, the emotion and, in many respects, upon that of others. You have observed that varying colors can make you feel this way or that. You have also observed that certain activities of merchandising employ certain combinations of colors and patterns to attract the attention and to inspire some latent quality, which would then enable the better sale of a product..."*

In all the past readings, Al occasionally would get a glimpse of the one for whom he was doing a reading outstretched before a group of individuals in an amphitheater, or he may have briefly seen the event he was giving the reading about. However, after that brief moment he was always then quickly enveloped by a mist and taken to a place of learning for him, far beyond.

When he returned from the reading, while he may occasionally have remembered short snippets of the scene he witnessed at the beginning, without listening to the recording, he would have no conscious recall of what was said in the remainder of the reading. If the reading were for an individual, he most often did not take the time to listen to it. He would simply package the tapes to send to his transcriber. If the reading were for one of his research projects, he would listen to it as soon as time would permit.

January 31 proved to be a significant change in this routine and the nature of his readings.

In the reading on this date, everything began as usual.

After his adjustments and closing his eyes, Al starts his journey through the welcoming darkness and into a gently undulating cloud of shimmering pastels, until the barely visible images of five or six individuals begin to take form before him.

Against the brilliance of the light coming from the opening of a great luminous tunnel, one of those individuals appearing before him is Lama Sing, who sits looking down into the tunnel past time and space to the reading room, speaking... *"Now, we would humbly take you into a journey which goes beyond the nature of the expressions of color on Earth as could be found either in the pigment or in the form of reflected or originated light."*

Al in spirit form, stands briefly behind Lama Sing, grasping his shoulder, a means of "grounding" him, so to say, giving him reference in the Beyond. He then turns to move with those accompanying him into the mist behind Lama Sing, expecting as usual to be taken beyond the reading to his place of learning. Instead, once in the mist, his movement (usually very rapid at this point) slows and the mist parts, revealing an expanse of green manicured lawn surrounding a three-story brick building. As he comes closer and closer to the brick wall of the structure, he is wondering what is going wrong in the reading, and whoosh... he has moved through the wall and is now traveling down the corridor of a pleasant-looking but aging hospital.

On the recording back in the reading room, Lama Sing is relating what is transpiring, *"We have before us now, through agreement, the activities and records of one whom we shall simply refer to as Peter..."*

Al continues down the hall—past a waiting room on the right, past the nurses' station, around a corner, and up to a room with a glass window and glass door. A nurse opens the door and Al finds himself moving into the room. There, beneath the covers of the bed, connected to the monitoring equipment, is the form of the man Lama Sing will begin referring to as Peter. Seated at his bedside is another man, appearing to Al to be in his late fifties or so. He is wearing baggy pants, a heavy-knit wide-collared cardigan with large buttons, his head capped with a yarmulke, and wrapped around his shoulders is a prayer shawl.

The narration resumes, *"Peter has come to the point of conclusion of a lifetime on Earth. During the course of his lifetime..."*

Al, hovering above the scene, doesn't hear Lama Sing. He is still wondering what is going on, feeling awkward, even invasive in witnessing the scene unfolding before him, Peter in and out of consciousness. The emotion in the room is thick, which Al feels to the core of his being.

Suddenly, Peter's eyes open and Al hears Peter speak to his friend, "We've had such good times, haven't we."

Al sees the friend look down and swallow hard to contain his grief, and then hears him reply, "We really have."

An attractive, well-groomed middle-aged woman enters the room. Al instantly knows she is Peter's beloved wife. He sees Peter become radiant at her presence, and notes that the love in the room between these three is almost tangible. There are further exchanges between the three, with Al all the while looking on incredulously, becoming captivated, feeling the impact of being a part of this event, experiencing it from within the heart of each one present.

He watches as Peter's wife bends down to place her lips beside her husband's face, whispering something to him. Al can see a peace steal throughout Peter and a smile appear as his eyes close.

After awhile, Peter's wife leaves the room, evidently an agreement between she and Peter that she not be present when the time comes.

There is silence now except for the monitors and the irregular breathing of one whose body is giving way.

The friend moves closer to the bed, gently grasping Peter's hand.

The silence intensifies.

Moments later, the tiny smile caused by his wife's whispered words still evident on his face, Peter begins his final journey beyond the room... beyond the hospital... beyond the portal called death, through the veil of darkness...

A short distance behind, Al follows, unseen, back into the darkness, the darkness that enveloped him in its loving neutrality as he began this reading.

Lama Sing continues, *"Peter begins to move with a fluidity likened unto that of a great bird soaring across an open azure sky. So it is that his spirit is now like this—a great silver-winged creature moving across the heavens."*

As Al's consciousness is returned to his body, details of the just concluded reading begin to flood his thoughts. He sits numbed, not moving, eyes closed, his mind stumbling over itself trying to grasp the reality that he is actually recalling it all, the first time this has happened in thousands of readings. Stunned at what he is remembering, he begins to question his sanity. Even for a guy who does readings for a living, this is bizarre. If he opens his eyes, what will he see — will it be his office or that hospital? He peaks through the slit of one eye. When he started the reading, it was daylight. Now, there is only darkness. Maybe he has he died and this was all somehow or other his own death experience. The room comes into dim focus from the glow of the night-light. Somewhat reassured by the familiarity of what he can see, that at least he is back where he started from, he reaches over and turns on a lamp and then the phone, to try to increase the sense of normalcy, as more and more of the specifics hit him.

How is any of this possible, he questions. And this man, Peter… what drew them together in that way. Maybe he's made too many trips to the Other Side. Maybe he shouldn't do the readings anymore. He decides there is no way he can send this reading out to the research group, who are expecting a reading on 'Colors.' He'll simply do another reading and set this one aside. The phone screams. He fumbles to bring it to his ear, relieved to hear a dear friend on the other end.

Bit by bit, Al launches into his experience, the friend's growing excitement beginning to infect Al as they consider the incredible opportunity for the research group, the insights that could be gathered about what happens when someone dies. To be able to follow Peter through the process of death into his travels beyond, and be able to ask questions along the way, paled the research they'd done to now. They couldn't wait to tell the others, and to get the next reading in what would come to be called, THE PETER PROJECT.

What you are about to read is the story of Peter's incredible life after he died, given by Lama Sing through Al Miner.

The words given are nearly verbatim; the dates beginning each chapter are the actual dates the readings were given.

As you consider what we are about to give, we would humbly suggest that you read not only with the mind, but also with the heart.

For what is contained is intended to inspire, and lead you to the recognition of your own potential... as it always has been, and ever shall be.

–Lama Sing

CHAPTER 1

Beyond the Blackness
JANUARY 31, 1990

We have before us now, through his agreement, the activities and records of one whom we shall simply refer to as "Peter."

Peter has come to the point of conclusion of a lifetime on Earth. During the course of his lifetime, we find that he has accomplished a significant state of balance. In terms of the Earthly records, he has been successful in his own enterprise. He has dealt with others in an honest and forthright manner, and with his family and friends in a loving and reliable way. In other words, for the most part, his lifetime in the Earth is significant as being the exemplification of that which is thought of as balance.

Peter is now concluding his life, and the body is being released. In the final stages of his dis-ease, his spirit had been apart from the body frequently.

There is little consciousness of what the body is now undergoing, no indicators of pain, at this current point. The feeling is one of restfulness, in addition to some anxiety, apprehension, and emotional uncertainty.

At his side have been his loved ones, including a dear friend who has been an inspiration throughout this life, one with whom he often bantered about varying points of view, philosophies, and such.

This friend, whom we'll call Abe, has a different faith. He believes in God, and though his friend is a Christian and he, himself, does not recognize Christ as the Messiah, this is not a barrier between them. His prayer and his love, and the memory of their many fond times together, reach out to embrace his friend – spiritually, emotionally, and even physically – as their hands touch in a final clasp of friendship.

It is the purity of this friendship that makes for a uniqueness in this time of movement for Peter from the Earth—the Christian and the Jew have come together and found a bridge of camaraderie, of a knowing that their heritage is from the one God, one and the same for both. That which is a point of contention for many on Earth has become meaningless for these two, for they are, in the finality, united in the spirit of true friendship.

Peter, as he removes from his physical body the final vestiges of the filament of light which is his spirit, and once again takes a journey as he oft did in prayer and meditative reverence, that in this experience he is fully cognizant of his movement.

In a moment of concern for the well-being of those left behind, a light passes through him which erodes all facets, every last granule, of this emotional energy from his being. It is not a light as you would see in your mind as we speak, of white or of brilliance; but it is a color of darkness, velvety, rich, perhaps best described as blackness.

What is this velvety rich indigo veil and does it have a purpose? One purpose is that this veil of darkness not only separates realms of consciousness and existence, but provides for a purification... provides, in a manner of speaking, a state of balance or ease between them. So as Peter passes through this veil of darkness, it is like an essence of God-like veil, like a living membrane, that enables him to suddenly realize that all that is being left behind is well and shall be well, and is held within the loving and protective embrace of God.

Now Peter begins experiencing incredible feelings of warmth and safety, as he slowly becomes conscious of the presence of someone with him. Though Peter hasn't fully recognized this other presence, the one accompanying him is one of Peter's guides, whom we'll call Paul.

Paul continues, as does Abe, now with tears falling from his cheeks, to hold Peter in an attitude of loving kindness. Here and there, Peter is abruptly jolted, as though his movement was being brought short by some tethers, some entwinement. It is in these moments that Abe is reaching out in sadness at the loss of his friend, Peter.

As Peter begins to wonder what this is, the presence of Paul becomes more and more evident, and because these are like loving filaments of light between Abe and Peter likened unto an umbilical cord of sorts, Paul is enabled to convey to Abe, through these filaments of light, a sense of well-being similar to what Peter has just been experiencing.

In an instant, Abe releases Peter's hand, strokes it gently, comments, "Goodbye, dear friend," and departs from the room.

With this, Peter begins to move with a fluidity likened unto that of a great bird soaring across an open azure sky. So it is that his spirit is now like this—a great silver-winged creature moving across the heavens.

Continually moving at Peter's side, Paul begins to envelop Peter with an orb of light meant to protect and shield him so that Peter might have this opportunity to deal with whatever Earthly thoughts, attitudes, and emotions might yet remain with him.

While this is moreso a protective mechanism, it also provides a state of balance, so that Peter's soul can accomplish a spiritual awakening in and of itself and in its own measure of time. When Paul endows Peter with this orb of light, he is actually embracing Peter with his spiritual cloak, or the power of his own spiritual awareness.

They are still within the realm which is called the Veil of Darkness, and though the feeling of movement continues, it is perceptibly slower. Peter is approaching a point of pause.

At this point, Peter becomes aware of himself and aware of the fact that he is continuing to exist. He becomes cognizant of the fact that he is no longer feeling the sensations that he did... the fatigue, the difficulty in his breathing, and all that sort, which is called (in this realm) "the Earthly heaviness".

As Peter discovers this and marvels at it, there is the gradual increase of what we'd call a luminosity. Time passes, as measured on Earth. Actually, it is the proceeding of the growth of awareness, rather than time.

Paul assesses the presence of Free Will and certain other Laws which are in action here, detecting them by the measure of the spirituality or literally by the observation of what you'd call the spiritual cloak of Peter. As Peter's awareness of his continued existence becomes keen enough, Paul begins to make himself and his presence known, finally stating rather loudly, "Hello, there."

Peter is startled just a bit. It doesn't quite register that someone else would be here, for he doesn't know, you see, where 'here' is. But he feels so good and so free of heaviness and pain and so alive, that he responds in kind, "Hi, there."

With this, the two of them simply look upon one another, with Paul generally doing the smiling and Peter generally doing the inquiring, not in a verbal sense but moreso in the countenance.

Taken back to speech once again, Peter asks questions such as, "Who are you, where am I, and what has happened?" and the conversation continues between them.

Essentially what is taking place is an explanation of what has transpired, and a continued time of balancing for Peter. Varying lengths of Earth-measured time can transpire at this point.

Generally, the explanations are dependent totally upon the spiritual consciousness of the entity and the realm of consciousness unto which they are to transcend. In this instance we have this one, Peter, who is quite balanced in terms of spiritual progression and has completed a lifetime without any karmic baggage to accompany him. So he is essentially given quite a considerable breadth of choice in terms of realms of consciousness. To state that to you in another manner—it will depend somewhat upon his ability to respond here, to recover, as to where he'll go to first.

Turning back to them, we find that they have reached an understanding of what has transpired—that the body has been left behind, and Paul, and several others who have come, have convinced Peter that he is quite fine and that life is going to continue.

There is a bit more luminosity now as the entire entourage has continued to drift—we'll use the reference point of upwards, for your understanding.

The general color around them at present has shifted from the deep dark color, a blue-back of sorts, to have moreso a brownish tinge, though around the group is a sort of luminosity, as though there is a source of light from within the group or collectively from within the sum total of the entities therein. This creates a sphere of light, then, that from a distance appears to be moving through this other substance of light or color, which is rather transparent, for the brownish color within can be seen clearly. They are moving, as we observe them, through this. And as they do, they are moving into an ever-lightening hue of this basic color.

Peter begins to notice his surroundings much more attentively now and looks over Paul's shoulder to see what lies beyond. He has become aware of the fact that they seem to be in motion, yet it does not appear that Paul is making an effort of any kind to accomplish that motion. Turning to Paul, he inquires about this.

"Remember, Peter," answers Paul, "you are not on Earth any longer, and though on Earth you might use your feet and legs or other modes of transportation to move from one place to another, here that is not necessary, though you may do so if you wish," at which point he offers to walk with Peter, if Peter would prefer.

Peter becomes introspective for a moment or two, causing the light around him to intensify. Paul stands back to allow him latitude, and Peter once again comes forth and asks, "Does it make a difference?"

Paul, struggling just a bit to contain a rather spontaneous outburst of good cheer and loving humor, measures his response, "No, I don't really think so. It is just a matter of choice."

So they concur and exchange further such verbal communications, and Peter observes that the color is becoming even lighter. As he looks into the color, he sees that there appear to be entities out there in the color.

Paul asks, "Do you wish to pause here?"

"Who are those people?" Peter asks. "Those are people over there, aren't they?"

Without looking, Paul affirms, "Yes."

"Well, don't they see us? Why don't they speak or acknowledge our presence?"

"No, as a matter of fact, they can't see us at all."

Again, as Peter processes this information he lights up, so to say, and Paul stands back, waiting until Peter is ready. Then they move on, Paul patiently continuing to answer Peter's questions.

They have moved now into a tan environment, though still, the light around them has been and continues to be white or clear. From outside the orb, it would be perceived as a wispy white; viewed from within, it would be seen as clear, as though there were no light around them at all, but a wispiness of whitish color circumferences them as they move.

Observing Peter's awareness of the light, Paul comments, "Yes, you may touch it, if you wish."

Peter ponders Paul's comment to his unspoken

thought, to which Paul responds, "Yes, if you pause a moment, you can hear me speak without listening, just as I can hear your thoughts without you speaking them."

Peter's reaction to that which Paul is telling him can perhaps be anticipated, as he immediately lights up in a brilliant silver-white ball. Paul, with delight, once again moves back to await Peter's digestion of that realization.

So it goes, and they move on until they have passed through the tan color and into the next, a very brilliant, very intense yellow. Due to the impact of this color upon Peter, their movement is a bit more rapid, until the color begins to moderate to a lovely, velvety feeling of creamy sunlight.

Peter comments, "My, how inspiring and cheering this color is after the brown."

"Wait until you see the next one."

Peter glows in anticipation, and once again, Paul stands back until Peter is balanced, and they continue their movement.

The yellow seems to give way here and there, with tinges of another color taking its place. They appear green, at first, ever so softly, and then with a brilliance and a force so as to be almost musical in their tonal quality, their hue, their brilliance. Again, the green becomes so intense that Peter reacts, and they accelerate their movement until the green shifts and becomes a soft pastel, like sunlight reflecting off a green meadow.

Now it seems as though the yellow has returned, and the green and yellow interplay produces a reaction within Peter of familiarity and fondness.

"You like these colors, don't you, Peter?"

"Yes, I really do," and looks deep into these expressions of light and vibration, that are not pigment nor particles of reflected light; they are like living expressions, much in the manner as one would press a key upon a piano and then the next and the next, all seem to be vibrating.

As Peter peers out into the color, again he notices entities, but this time they have stopped whatever it is they are about and seem to be observing, or at least looking in Peter's direction.

Peter asks immediately, "You said the others didn't see me. Do these people see me?"

"Yes, they do know we're here, though they don't completely see us."

Adjusting quickly to this thought, Peter asks further, "Well, what do they see?"

"They see our light."

"What light?"

"The light of our spiritual consciousness."

"What's that?"

"Well, it's just something that you have. It's sort of like abilities or talents on Earth, or hair color."

"What color is my hair, anyway?"

"What color do you want it to be? It's just the same as it was on Earth, Peter."

They continue their discussion in this manner for a time until Paul asks, "Are you comfortable here, or would you like to go on?"

Peter pauses a moment and studies the entities, who seem pleasant, noting that they are not paying much attention to his presence.

After a brief time, Paul suggests, "Wouldn't you like to continue on a bit further and see what lies ahead?" Mindful that he shouldn't lead Peter too heavily, knowing his task as a guide is a delicate one requiring some attention to a fine line of balance, he follows this with, "But if not, we can certainly stay here."

They conclude that a bit more movement wouldn't hurt, and off they go.

The next color encountered by Peter seems to shed a bluish cast over what was previously about them. As the blue begins to become more visible, however, it just as quickly gives way to red.

At first, the red is subtle. Then with a thump, it intensifies, causing a jolt to Peter's consciousness. "This is not good," says Peter, and Paul responds with actions to preserve and protect his companion. They move more swiftly and a dilution of the intensity of the red takes place.

All the while, Paul is observing Peter's reactions. Once again Peter sees several entities off to the left, up on what appears to be a mound of greener color, like a green hillside. Startled by the fact that one of them raises a hand and gestures as though waving at him, impulsively he raises his hand and waves back. The one upon the summit nods, turns, and seems to continue walking. Peter can't see where.

The other two with him didn't even wave, Peter thinks to himself. *Not very courteous.*

Knowing Peter's thoughts, Paul responds, "No, that's not it at all. They simply couldn't quite make you out. The tall one with the book in his arm is their guide."

"What do you mean, 'guide'? Are they on a tour?"

Paul sparkles with humor, and responds lovingly. "You could call it such, though it is more of a variation on that theme."

Peter looks around and notes objects that appear to be forms of vegetation, plants and greenery. "Where are we?"

"At a new level of consciousness, you might say. Would you like to rest?"

Peter considers this carefully and then responds, "No, I don't think so. It seems somehow too heavy for me here. Does that make sense to you?"

"Indeed it does," responds Paul, and off they go again.

Here, again, the color begins to change, and as it does, Peter changes as well. Paul is carefully observing Peter's reactions. The indigo is returning, and Peter is giving indications of being weary.

They continue a bit in the darkness and, to Paul's expectation, Peter falls asleep.

The colors Peter passed through were representations of the varying strata of emotions, memories, and thought-forms which remained with him as vestiges from his most recent life on Earth. The changing hues and intensity of the colors were indications of the degree of their continued effect upon him. He encountered himself on multiple levels, though he knew himself not... at least not yet.

When he explored these at multiple levels of consciousness, he became fatigued, having reached the highest level he was able to accept at that point. Peter's sleep is not a sleep in the sense as known on Earth. He is not sleeping to restore his physical body. He is, rather, in a sleep of spirit; he has moved within himself for a period of balance

The entity who gestured to him is in fact the spirit of Abe, his friend. So Peter's emotion was mixed. The bond between Abe and Peter, now out of physical body, was completed on another level of consciousness.

Consider this: in Peter we can find the reflection of ourselves. For, through the processing of our experiences, do we all come to a greater comprehension of who and what we are. It is through the progression of an array of experiences, including incarnations on Earth, that we weave the fabric of our very being.

CHAPTER 2

In the Garden Realm
MARCH 29, 1990

During his spiritual rest, Peter was given an opportunity to review not only his just-previous incarnation in the Earth, but he was also afforded a comparative analysis of sorts of all of his past experiences which have involved the Earth and certain other realms, to the degree which his own consciousness is capable of accepting.

As a part of that activity, many entities were present, providing reference, providing assistance, and, of course, as ever, supporting, protecting, and nurturing any need that Peter might have had. Throughout the process, Paul was present and certainly knowledgeable of what was taking place. In addition to this, there were the opportunities given to re-examine the just-previous lifetime based upon the influences or you might call them emotions, memories, thought-forms, which remained as vestiges of a sort even as he proceeded into these realms.

The luminosity about Peter, now, is brilliant, and the movement of varying colors throughout the orb enveloping him has subsided somewhat. From this we can interpret that he has come to a point of balance and understanding from which he can now resume his exploration with Paul.

As Peter stirs, the brilliance of his envelopment changes perceptibly, becoming more translucent. Paul nods a warm greeting to Peter, which actually is a collection of directed thought-forms. It appears as a collage of color, and is accompanied, as always in these realms, by a resonance of sound or music.

The combination of this color and its resonance (as it were, music) has an immediate impact upon Peter, and he feels as though he is returning to the presence of an old and dear friend.

They spend a short period discussing his spiritual rest, and Peter inquires, "Are you aware of what I have just learned and experienced, Paul?"

"Yes, I am. While in a state of rest, you have been coming to an understanding of what has been happening with you since having left your lifetime on Earth."

Peter then asks many questions in rapid succession, and as Paul begins to answer, their consciousness conjoins, and Paul has, once again, enveloped Peter with his own cloak of spirituality.

Finally, Peter asks, "What happens next?"

Paul, with some visible delight, evidenced by intensities or sparkles in his own luminosity, answers, "What would you *have* happen next?"

Peter pauses a moment and shifts slightly inward, again perceptible by the intensification and then diminishment of light in his cloak. "Whatever is appropriate."

"Wise choice. Shall we move on, then?"

Peter responds affirmatively, the combination of his apprehension and curiosity evidential in his cloak's activity.

Their movement is not measured in the same sense as it was previously. It is not a movement through different realms or strata of color or vibration. It is moreso defined as a lateral movement. Each separate realm of consciousness has its own protective envelopment, which could be called a veil of darkness, and Paul and Peter are now moving around within this veil of darkness, between realms. Peter continues his questioning, all the while keeping a cautious eye about himself, looking for anything which might seem familiar.

Paul is explaining various aspects of consciousness. "Each soul moves to a level of awareness which is essentially the equivalent of that soul's ability to accept. Therefore, you could surmise from that, that where you are is where you are willing to be."

Peter asks, "Just where is that? I mean, is it a place, or a location in the universe? You know, like in the evening sky? Am I near a certain planet, or what?"

Paul, with just a sparkle of understanding, answers, "Well, yes, you are, in essence, potentially at least, in all of those. In other words, dependent upon what we should choose as our focal point, we can be in any one of those."

Peter's robe lights up brilliantly, and Paul realizes that he has not conveyed completely the thought-form that is needed by Peter. When Peter's cloak calms a bit, he asks simply, "What?"

Paul gestures and suggests that Peter seat himself.

The thought of seating himself startles Peter a bit, but as he looks behind him, he sees that there is a beautiful bench. Looking around further, he sees that, not only is there the bench, but also surroundings of greenery, flowers, water trickling over several rocks into a fountain-like pool of water, and several other entities also seated across the way.

In disbelief, Peter turns quickly back to Paul, whose appearance now has also changed to be that of a much more visible, a much more definable or, in short, a very real person. Peter again, of course, shifts inwardly, and for a moment or two is only perceptible as a brilliant light. Cautiously returning to a level of communication with Paul, he asks, "Where are we? What has happened?"

Paul smiles and states, "Let's have a seat and we can discuss this at great length, if you wish. Quite a pleasant spot, wouldn't you say, Peter?"

Peter becomes more comfortable and seats himself and begins to observe what is about him, realizing that it is, indeed, warm and pleasant. The odors are sweet and alive. The atmosphere is filled with lovely, pure, familiar colors. He can hear the song of creatures off in the distance, though he sees them not... familiar to him as songbirds and the like. There is a wind gently perceptible, and it has the effect of making him feel marvelous, as though it passes directly through him eroding any sense of apprehension, doubt, fear, or fatigue.

Turning to look back at the pool, upon its surface he sees a slight reflection of the light about the perimeter here and there. Within the water are luminous spots of light, which, as he focuses upon them, he can perceive as fish. Looking to its expanse (for it is quite great in its semi-circular shape) he notes the presence of brilliantly colored water flowers and sees in its center a projection of hewn stone, marble-like in appearance, from which water cascades downward, giving off almost a musical cascade of sound, as it does—not so as to be obtrusive but, rather, gently blending with all the other fragrances, colors, sounds, light, and other sensations he seems incapable of defining at present.

He turns his gaze back to his companion, Paul, who is seated at arm's-length next to him on the semi-circular bench, and looks into his eyes for a moment or two. What he sees is gentleness, love, compassion, understanding all focused there now. So marvelous are the feelings that radiate from Paul's eyes, that Peter is near speechless in wonder.

Paul, understanding completely, and knowing Peter's thoughts, speaks softly to him. "Are you comfortable, Peter? Is this pleasant for you? Do you need anything?"

"I am very comfortable, and it would appear I need nothing." Then, looking about, he asks, "What is this place?"

"Well, actually, it was created some time ago by friends of yours."

"Friends of mine? What friends?"

"They are members of a group of which you also are a

member, and who have been in part observing and experiencing with you, during your just-previous activity on Earth."

After a sparkling moment or two of introspective analysis, Peter responds, "I see. And who exactly is this group, and why am I a member of it? Is it like a club or a lodge or a fraternity, such as I knew on Earth?"

Mirthfully, Paul answers, "In a manner of speaking. However, you have belonged to this group for a great deal of time. Remember your experiences during your rest period, of viewing other lifetimes on Earth?"

Peter reflects a moment, then replies, "Yes. Why, I had almost forgotten all of that. It's as though it was absorbed into my being somehow and no single memory seemed to stand out; but as you question me, I do recall it. Are you saying that I have been a member of this group back through all those other experiences?"

Paul simply smiles and nods.

Peter considers this for just a moment and the barrage of questions begins again. "What kind of a group is this? Does it have to do with who and what I am now? I mean I seem to be just as I was on Earth. Am I?"

"For the moment you are, Peter, but you don't need to stay that way unless you prefer to. The group is called your 'soul group', and you have been with them since the beginning of your involvement with Earth and realms like it. Do you understand, Peter?"

"Yes, I think so. It seems very complex and vast and, to an extent, impossible."

With that comment, Paul's humor spills forth, and as he laughs aloud at Peter's response, Peter notes with wonder that he has perceived the laughter as coming from within himself as much as hearing it coming from Paul. "Goodness, Paul. When you laughed just then, I could feel that humor inside of me, almost as though I was laughing with you or, rather, that it echoed inside of me. What is that? And how is it that this wind or breeze or whatever it is seems to be blowing through me and making me feel as I do?"

Paul pauses a moment and becomes a bit more focused. As he looks again at Peter, he answers, "Your expression at this moment, Peter, is not physical in the sense of having bone and flesh, but it is physical in the sense of being a primary thought-form. A primary thought-form exists, as does the physical, in that it occupies space. It has density. It has the capacity to function as a thing. Therefore, when it is expressed in a realm such as this, it becomes all-inclusive. In other words, you are capable of experiencing all of the aspects of this place, this realm… as you are doing right now. So what occurs about you also occurs within you."

Peter is again illuminated, as he turns inward to digest what Paul has just given him.

When his cloak dims in its intensity, Paul suggests, "Would you like to perform a small experiment, to demonstrate what I've just conveyed to you?"

With measured exuberance tempered by apprehension, Peter answers, "Well, I guess so. What is it?"

"Turn about, and reach your hand into the pool of water behind you."

Dutifully, Peter turns, extends his hand, slips it into the water, and quickly retrieves it. Looking at his hand and the water on it, he turns back to Paul, "What is this? It looks like water, it has the characteristics of water, but it's not at all similar to the experience on Earth of placing my hand in water. Not at all."

"How would you describe it, Peter?"

"Well, it's as though the water and my hand became sort of tied together. Instead of feeling an immediate coolness or difference in temperature and the feeling of wetness, I felt something else."

Smiling just a bit, Paul asks, "What do you think that something else was?"

"I have no idea. It just felt... good."

"Good in what way?"

"Well, it felt as though the water was reaching out to hold my hand as I was reaching out to immerse my hand within it, and as I had my hand in the water, it seemed to become one with my hand. In other words, there wasn't any difference in temperature. You know, water's usually cool when it sits like that. This water felt just right."

Looking at the water again, Peter goes on. "It's different than water as I've known it... like it's alive, like it has resonance... like I'm putting my hand into a container of color and sound and... well, happiness."

Paul, steadily observing Peter, makes contact with his eyes and simply nods. "That's it, Peter. You've got it. All that is in this realm, and yourself, are as one. What you feel when you place your hand in the water is yourself. You are all of the things that you have just used to describe the sensation, the feeling of the water."

There is a period of reflection as Peter attempts admirably not to dwell on the specifics, but rather, to grasp the big picture, the overview.

He turns to look at Paul, and asks, "What you are saying, then, is that in essence, where I am and who I am are all one, all the same. In other words, it's sort of like..."

There is a very long pause as Peter searches for the right words to express himself.

Paul interjects gently, "Peter, you needn't try to express what you feel with words. For I know what you are attempting to say. I can feel your thought-form. Therefore, describing it to me is secondary."

This seems to be a relief to Peter, for his struggle to fully express in words what he was truly experiencing was almost beyond his ability. The terminology, the words, the interpretations and their accompanying meanings seem to be distant, almost as though they belong somewhere else.

They communicate like this for some time, discussing many things of this same nature.

As they do so, Peter becomes aware of the presence of other entities once again, who are seated on a knoll some distance away. "Could you tell me who those people are over there?"

Paul, without looking, answers, "They're friends of yours, Peter. They are also members of that soul group I was telling you about."

"You mean I know them? That is... I did know them? Or... they know me? Or we were together back there?"

Paul once again sparkles with loving humor. "Yes."

Unable to take his eyes off the entities, Peter asks with a hint of uncertainty, "Well, could I meet them? I mean, could you introduce me to them?"

"Of course, Peter, if that is your wish. Would you like to go over to them, or would you like me to bring them over here to you?"

Remembering his Earthly manners, "Well, whatever is appropriate. I mean, there doesn't appear to be enough seating here," and as Peter turns about to confirm that there is only the one bench that he and Paul are seated on, it is with some surprise that he notes that several other benches are now present, each one as beautiful and as ornately carved as the one upon which he is seated.

Paul now brings the three entities over to Peter and introduces them in a formal method acceptable to Peter's experience from Earth, and they are in discussion, spontaneously invoked by the tallest of the three, one of the two females.

She has reddish or auburn hair and her smile causes Peter to feel a sense of compassion and understanding emanating from her very being.

She asks Peter a number of questions about how he feels, whether or not he finds the realm in which he is now present a pleasant one, what he thinks of the workmanship of the benches and some of the carvings, whether or not the flowers some distance away are those which he might have chosen, and all that sort.

As she does, the others have seated themselves and are simply observing and nodding, smiling, just as casually as any group might converse in the Earth.

A mesmerized Peter is smiling and nodding to the one's questions, which he doesn't really hear. *It's like a beam of sunlight each time she smiles*, he thinks to himself.

The male entity of the three now leans forward and asks Paul, "Did you have a good journey here?"

"Indeed, Zachary, it was pleasant enough, and interesting." Turning to Peter, "Didn't you think so, Peter?"

Peter's spell is broken, and he is disarmed by Paul's question since he has nothing to compare it to. "Yes… yes, I guess it was."

Playfully, Zachary asks Peter, "Do you have anything you would like to do? If you don't have anything in particular in mind, I would be pleased to show you about the grounds."

Peter startles himself by answering, "Why yes, I would like to see more of this place. It is mysteriously beautiful, and intriguing."

Without another word, Zachary rises, takes Peter's arm, and leads him away from the group.

Peter turns quickly, casting an anxious eye back at Paul, who seems at this point to him to be his only line of security, his only real friend.

Paul simply smiles and nods, waving his arm as though to say… go ahead, you're alright.

At this point, the others – the two females and Paul – look at one another and begin to communicate.

The smaller of the two females retrieves a book.

Peter has discovered that he is much more than a physical being. He has passed through a period of evaluation (his spiritual sleep), which allowed him to understand and make himself complete—or at least, as complete as he is willing to accept at this point. After which, Paul took him on a somewhat lateral course in that level of consciousness to this place, this Eden-like garden, wherein they have had this exchange and these experiences.

Understand that Peter is beginning to awaken. In other words, one might think in his departure from Earth that the term you call death is to fall into a sleep. To a degree, as we indicated to you through Peter's experiences, that is so. But it is not an eternal sleep, nor is it ever a sleep which is without consciousness. It is the transference or shifting of the focal point of consciousness from one position to another. All of the expressions in this place are those which are the equivalent of acceptable levels of existence within Peter. The pool of water, the flowers, the bushes, the sky, the Earth, the entities, the bench—are all acceptable to him. In fact, they are high levels of acceptability within Peter. Another way of expressing this is to say that they are levels of anticipation within Peter... some of the highest he has ever had.

The exploration of this level of expression is an important step in the progression of the soul known to you as Peter. Whether or not Peter shall proceed beyond this point is totally Peter's decision.

CHAPTER 3

About God
MARCH 29, 1990

In the beginning was The Word. And The Word was with God.

So it is, dear friends, that from this we can learn to understand the true nature of God's existence. As we consider the meaning of the expression "The Word," we can come to understand that this is the essence of what could be called a thought-form.

A thought-form is an expression of creative potential and power, the sum total of which was in the beginning with God. Another way of stating this would be to say that the entire potential for all of existence was in residence within the consciousness of God, not as yet outwardly expressed in the form of His Word or thought.

About God—as many as there are eyes to see, to perceive, so then as well might there be an equal number of interpretations or perspectives about God. While the information which shall follow may strain some concepts just a bit here and there, it is our humble prayer that this will not be beyond the level of tolerance, but sufficient so as to awaken and cause the desire for further seeking or searching.

Zachary and Peter have returned from their travels about the Garden Realm and have been in discussion with Paul and the others.

Peter asks, "What is the book you have there?" thinking to himself that this is the first evidence of any printed word or manufactured item.

Peter joins the others, sitting on the empty bench, joyful from his tour. "Well, it was, as Zachary said, splendid. This place is really beautiful." He notices that Elizabeth still has the book in her lap, and once again, tries to get a better look at it. Thinking to himself that this is the first evidence he has noticed of any printed word, he finally asks, "What is the book you have there?"

The entity looks at Peter, again with the warmth of understanding and compassion as previously, and responds simply, "Peter, this is a book which contains knowledge from what is called the Hall of Records. It holds the answers to your questions, and is specifically present because it is intended for you and you alone."

Reflecting upon those words, Peter draws inward just a bit, causing his spiritual cloak to sparkle.

Paul is the first to speak next. "Peter, take a few moments to reflect upon who and where you are. Then, if any questions should come to you, why not express them, and we'll see just what she is attempting to tell you."

After considering this for a moment, Peter answers, "Great idea. How about that book telling me about God?"

Without a moment's hesitation, she gently taps the book, opens it, and responds, "God is the essence of your very being. Although you might not think it so, you are as much God as God is you. In other words, you and God are inseparable."

There is silence for a time as Peter attempts to digest that morsel of information, and responds, "What does that mean? Are you saying that I am God? That sounds a bit like blasphemy, doesn't it? I mean, how could I ever consider myself to be God? Look at all of the flaws I have, the faults. I didn't do all that great in the experience I just left. Oh, sure, I didn't do too badly, but nothing outstanding. How can you expect me to believe what you have just said?"

"Well, if God is within you and you are within God, then the potential of God's creative power and grace must also be within you. True?"

"Well, I suppose so. But how can you prove that? How can I understand that without some evidence?"

"Why don't you try another experiment? Simply do this. Close your senses. In other words, close your eyes, close down your hearing, and all that, and let yourself be free."

After a brief struggle, Peter finds it remarkably easy to attain a state in which he feels as though he is suspended, floating, just having a wonderful sensation of being unrestricted. Dimly, he can hear Paul say, "Now have a thought."

Have a thought? Peter thinks to himself. *What in the world does he mean, 'have a thought'?*

Even though Peter hadn't spoken aloud, Paul answers. "Think of a flower, or twenty flowers, if you will."

Instantly, Peter's mind fills with images of beautiful purple-petaled flowers with yellowish-gold centers, perched atop strong slender stalks, bearing a few symmetrical leaves.

Again, he hears Paul dimly, as though they are separated by a considerable distance, "Now, Peter, return to your state here with us. Awaken and let your senses be regained."

Dutifully, Peter responds, though with some effort. Upon opening his eyes, he looks upon this little group, who all seem to be gently and supportively watching him.

"What did you see, Peter?" Paul asks.

Excitedly, Peter answers, "Well, listen to this. I not only saw, but I smelled and felt and heard beautiful purple flowers with golden..." and at that word, he notices that extending beyond the benches upon which they are seated, is a vast expanse of the very flowers he had just described. Incredulous, he asks, "How did they get there? Where did they come from? Those are the very flowers I had imagined."

Each of the others sparkles a bit around the fringes of their own spiritual cloaks.

Zachary comments, "Well now, it would appear that you must have had some effect with your thought, and with the power of your own presence, in order for these flowers to be here. Or perhaps you might convince yourself that in the few moments while you were resting, we four very rapidly went forth, gathered the flowers, planted them, and seated ourselves back here without you knowing we were gone."

All five chuckle at the absurdity of this thought.

Silence follows as Peter gazes at the expanse of purple, watching as the flowers seem to each be expressing some unique facet of the color or hue of their own being.

Zachary again breaks the silence, stating to the one with the book, "Why don't you help Peter understand what took place, since you are holding the book."

With a smile she responds, "Peter, as the book informed you, you and God are one. So, as you focused without reservation upon these beautiful flowers, God also focused upon them and saw that they were good, and that they were of pleasure to you and to Him. In that moment of simultaneity, of a mutuality of love, of appreciation, and of wonder, so then did these flowers come into existence."

Peter mentally chews on those words, striving to break them down into more digestible mental morsels.

Zachary, meanwhile, is becoming more and more obviously uninvolved in the conversation... looking off into the distance, then looking up, then over his shoulder, crossing his legs and clasping his hands over one knee, generally looking as though he is quite bored.

Since Zachary and Peter have become somewhat close during their journeys through this garden, Peter is comfortable questioning Zachary about this, "What's wrong, Zack? You don't seem to be impressed or interested in what's taken place here with these flowers."

Zachary turns abruptly, as though he were just called from a daydream, and answers, "Flowers? What flowers?"

"Why, those flowers right over…" Where the flowers were, is a beautiful, undulating field of lush green grass, waving and swaying to a gentle breeze. "What happened to my flowers?" stammers Peter. "They… they're gone!"

"So as ye believe," Paul answers, "so is it. So as you are willing to accept, so is it given you. So as you have doubt, then doubt diminishes the power and the durability of the thought-form which you build. The presence of God within you, or any entity, is diminished, clouded, veiled, filtered, by the action of doubt or fear."

Visibly disappointed and shaken by the loss of his accomplishment, Peter looks from one to the other of his new friends. First to Zachary, who again is looking away in a manner which seems disinterested, and then back to Paul, who has just the tiniest trace of a grin on one corner of his mouth.

Peter sighs, "Well, apparently, from what you're suggesting, my questioning, my incredulous reaction to the appearance of these flowers, somehow or other caused them to vanish. Am I to conclude from that, then, that they were merely an illusion? You know, a daydream or a figment of whatever imagination and mind I have left here?"

This brings an outpouring of humor from the group, but no one speaks.

Peter looks from one to the other, and each in turn looks away as his gaze falls upon them. Zachary is again fidgeting, looking down, looking up, almost to the point of getting up and walking away.

"Say, Zack," Peter asks, "what in the world is troubling you, anyway?"

Turning to Peter, with a look of embarrassment, Zachary replies, "What's that, Peter? Sorry. Must have drifted off there a bit. Were you speaking to me?"

"Yes. What's troubling you? What is bothering you? It seems as though you're not even with us here. Is this something that displeases you, or what?"

"Oh, not at all, Peter. I'm enjoying this very much. Sorry to have given you any indication that it was otherwise. I just have a lot on my mind these days. Lots of things I need to do, and lots of responsibilities, and I can't help but mull them over. They keep coming back to my mind. Sort of like a melody you've heard once a while ago, or an image or picture that, even though you put it out of your mind, back it comes. Know what I mean, Pete?"

After a moment's pause, Peter answers, "Well, yes, as a matter of fact, I do, Zack. Take those flowers. I keep seeing them in my mind's eye and..." with that, Peter notices that the flowers are once again scattered across the little knoll from where Peter sits with his friends. "Hey, look, everyone, the flowers are back! Look... they're back!" Without a moment's hesitation, he jumps to his feet and rushes over and throws himself into the array of flowers. "They are real! Look here! They're everywhere. Soft, velvety, smell so good, too. And the color... it seems to rub off on you. Makes me feel sort of... purple, just like them!"

Laughter abounds, as one might agitate an entire line of glass wind chimes... a tinkling, melodious sound.

With that, Zachary goes over to Peter and throws himself upon the flowers as well. "That's it, Peter. That's what was bothering me. I just needed some of this purple. Goodness, you certainly are perceptive. Knew just what I needed. Thanks very much, my friend."

With that, the remainder of the group, break out in spontaneous joy once again.

Nestled in the midst of this array of purple, swaying flowers, Peter sits up, crosses his legs, and Zachary imitates him. There they sit, nearly knee to knee, looking at one another.

"Well, Zack," Peter comments, nodding his head, "I get the feeling you set me up for this. Right?"

Zachary looks him in the eye and grins, "Well, in a manner of speaking. I was simply following orders. That book she's got... it's quite powerful, and... uh... one needs to be mindful of whom one is serving."

Peter, though he doesn't understand all of what Zachary has said, laughs a bit. "Well, no doubt you all have some intended lesson for me. Is that true?"

With that, all rise and join Zachary and Peter in the midst of the purple flowers.

"You see, Peter, belief in God is not as difficult as it might seem," explains Paul, "neither is the comprehension of God as difficult as it might seem. In order to understand something, it is better for one to experience it than to be told about it, to read about it, or to observe another whom is experiencing same. So it was believed to be best for you that you experience the extremes of your potential of believing. Since you asked the question about God, we felt this was a beautiful little example to illustrate to you what was meant by the Book of Wisdom in its answer to you."

Peter reflects for a moment, as the entire group becomes comfortable, touching the flowers, inhaling their fragrance, all of them generally taking on the purple glow being mysteriously being cast off by the flowers themselves.

Without plucking it, Peter takes a flower loosely in the palm of his hand. As he touches the petals and the center of the flower with his thumb, he reflects, "You know... I get the impression from looking at and touching this flower that it is somewhat like God. Correct me if I'm wrong, but from what you've shown me, I'm like one petal on this flower attached to God at the center. At the outer edge, I might think of myself as being independent from the center. Yet, if I allow my consciousness to run back to the center, I would realize that I am a part of this one creation, this one existence. Then, as well, I might see that there are other petals springing forth from the center." Peter pauses, thinking about what he has stated, marveling at his own insight.

Paul responds to Peter's thought, "It shouldn't surprise you to have such an insight, Peter. For look to your side and you'll see the book is adjacent to you."

Looking down to his right, Peter sees that the book has been carefully placed at his side. Looking back up at Paul again, searchingly, he asks, "Paul, are you telling me that simply because this book is next to me... in other words, in the general proximity of my physical... oops, scratch that... my... whatever being... that because of that, I'm wiser?"

Immediately Paul responds, "Yes."

"Well, now, Paul, how can that be? It's just a book, isn't it? After all, I've owned lots of books, and they never did anything like this for me. More often than not, I had to pore over them to extract anything lasting, and when I did, it only seemed to be productive after I applied it."

"Just the same here," answers Paul.

"Well, so you are saying that this book, just by being near me, makes me smarter?"

The group chuckles a bit, casting their light like little rivulets of brightly colored lights to dance across the tops of the flowers.

Peter notes that occurrence, and thinks to himself, *I'll have to ask about that sometime. Amazing!*

Paul speaks again, "Zachary, why don't you tell him what it's all about?"

Zachary, looking at Paul, answers, "Do you think I can, Paul?"

"Oh, I'm sure of it. I have every faith in you."

"Well, if you say so, Paul." Turning to Peter with a whimsical look on his face, "Peter, do you think I'm wise enough to answer your question?"

Peter was somewhat embarrassed and flustered at the directness of Zachary's question and, wanting to support his friend and be gracious, stammers, "Well, uh... uh... sure, I guess so, Zack. I mean, I've only just met you but you seem very bright."

Zachary, still with that look, answers, "Well, if you think I am, Peter, I'll give it a try. Look here, Pete, when you slipped your fingers around the flower you had a... what you called... an insight, didn't you?"

"Why, yes, I did, Zack."

"And where do you suppose that insight came from?"

"Well... Paul says it came from the book."

"Without what Paul said, Pete... where do *you* think the insight came from?"

Understanding that Zachary is once again trying to encourage him to make a discovery, Peter willingly reflects, looking down at the flower which he still holds loosely between his fingers and upon which his thumb once again now comes to rest. "Why, I believe, Zack, that the flower gave me that knowledge. Could that be true? Anyway, that's the thought that just came to my mind."

"Interesting. Just how did it come into your mind, do you think?"

Looking at him, Peter is obviously puzzled.

"Well, Pete, look at it this way... at what point did the thought come to you? Before or after you placed your thumb back on the center of the flower?"

"Well, it seemed to be just at that same instant as I touched the center of the flower." There is silence as Peter reflects upon his own words. Turning to Zachary again, he ventures, "Are you saying that, when I placed my thumb upon its center, this flower somehow or other conveyed that insight to me?"

"Well, after all... I'm not that wise, Pete... but it sure seems that way, doesn't it? All the indicators are there. You didn't have the thought before then."

"You're right! I think you're right. I think this flower was able somehow to connect with my mind. Now, how could it do that?"

Zachary, still whimsically grinning, casts a sideways glance back up at Peter, teasing, "Well, you're the one who created them …not me."

The words strike the core of Peter's being. "Oh, Zachary. This means that if I created these… no, scratch that… if God and I created these, then it stands to reason that a part of me and a part of God must also be within this very flower."

With that, Zachary now turns face-on to Peter, and states softly, "Bravo, my lad. Well done."

Having so stated, he rises and strides over to the bench, where he begins to casually straighten his spiritual cloak, as though he were no longer interested in participating.

Peter and Paul commence a discussion which will continue for a considerable length of time. It has to do with the nature of mind and spirit – not in the sense of the Earth plane, but in the sense of infinity – and in the course of this conversation, many things will be discussed. Among them, the varying aspects by which one can determine the nature and presence of God's spirit and thought, and how to function in accord with and in harmony with His presence.

Peter made a discovery that, when placing himself in a state of oneness with God, he can become a co-creator with God.

Thereafter, he also discovered that where he had a moment of doubt, question, or fear, his part of that creation broke down, so that his projection (which contributed to the expression of that creation in his realm) was no longer being sustained. The beautiful flowers continued to exist, but their expression of existence was no longer perceptible by Peter.

If you seek to know about God, understand from this little sharing with our good friends and colleagues and our ward, Peter, that to be a co-creator with God is an honor. That honor is supported by your faith; it is undermined by your doubt and by your fear.

If you wish to know about God, then do His work, and see that, as there are many flowers afield—each having many petals, each petal an expression of the center of existence, which is God—so as God's Word is expressed into consciousness, so are you expressed as being of God. You are His Word, His thought, His living expression.

You cannot be lost nor altered, for each of you are unique, and in that uniqueness does God find eternal beauty. As each flower afield, He knows them, every one.

CHAPTER 4

Co-creating
JUNE 3, 1990

Children have the beauty of all creation as the potential of their mind. In the sense that their mind has not been confined in any significant extent by those forces which could be called carnal, or Earthly, then it is from this perspective that one can understand and see more clearly than perhaps the average individual on Earth who has endured such conditioning.

So, when next a child might ask of you, "Where is... what is... how is... (and et cetera) ...God?" then answer quite simply in this way, "What do you think the answer to your question is?" Then, settle back and listen, and learn to see without limitation.

Any answer that would be given to a child would be, more likely than not, followed by at least two additional questions; and appropriately so, for the greater one has a comprehension of that which is limitless, the moreso does one seek to understand more about such limitlessness.

P eter and Paul are striding along a pathway in the Garden Realm, which they have been exploring for some period of time.

Peter is seeking understanding about the experience he has just had wherein he, as he was told, co-created along with the power of God a field of beautiful flowers.

"Paul, what actually took place? I mean, what was the mechanism that permitted me to... well, create... you know... to make those flowers become real?"

Paul motions with a sweep of his hand towards an ornate bench off to the side and they seat themselves. "You see, Peter, here… now… where we are, there is the potential which is not limited by what you would consider on Earth to be certain constraints. These constraints are not literally barriers or walls or such as you would think of them, implied by the term 'constraints' but they are nonetheless every bit as demarcating and constrictive as the term does imply. See?"

After some thought, Peter responds, "What do you mean? I didn't see any barriers on Earth that I can recall, other than having a few tough times here and there. Is that what you're talking about?"

Looking Peter squarely in the eye, Paul nods ever so slightly, and then looks off towards the distance where the azure blue sky merges into a collage of colors. "Moving together in harmony, things can work wonders; moving together in limitation, things can be particularly burdensome, obscuring… blocking." With that, he turns back to Peter, "Understand what I mean?"

Peter fidgets about and then looks back at Paul. "Well, no, not really. Could you be a bit more explicit?"

"Certainly, Peter. For example, take this bench we're seated on. Put your hand on it and tell me what you feel."

Dutifully, Peter feels the bench. "Well, it feels firm, it has some form. I… I don't know what is it you want me to say here, Paul."

Paul continues encouragingly, "Just what you said, but with greater perception and description. What do you feel? What do you sense? Try again."

This time, looking down at the bench, Peter studies it. He notes that the edges are perfectly beveled, as though some craftsman of remarkable skill has fashioned it. He notes the grain and pattern. It seems as though it is marble or something similar. He notes the curve as it moves around behind them, and here he runs his hand along the edge.

Instead of feeling what he anticipated – coldness, sharpness – a tingling sensation races up his hand from his fingertips, so startling him that he nearly jerks his hand away, but his curiosity causes him to stay with it, to continue to feel and sense these energies.

"This is very strange, Paul. Did you know I would have this strange sensation? Is that why you told me to touch the bench again?"

"I had hoped you would."

"Well, what *is* this that I feel? It's certainly not anything like what I would anticipate. My memory of a marble or stone bench is that it would be cold, and would be smooth in places and perhaps rough in others, and generally... you know... just *there*. Not anything other than just there. This bench doesn't seem to have that feel to it. It feels to me as though it's..."

Paul breaks the silence, "In motion? Alive? Warm?"

"Yes, yes! All those... and something else I can't quite define to you, Paul. It seems to almost electrify my hand and arm as I am in contact with it."

Neither Peter nor Paul had noticed the approach of Zachary, who is suddenly standing before them, gently rocking back and forth on his heels. "Ahem," he says boldly. "What are you two fellows up to? Taking a break, are you?"

With a start, Peter jumps to his feet. "Oh, hello, Zack. You certainly are a quiet one. I didn't hear you approach."

"Didn't mean to startle you, Pete. I'll make a note of that and make a bit of noise for you next time. So, what's up with you two here? What are you doing?"

"We were just talking about the nature of creation, and mind and spirit, Zachary," answers Paul, "using this bench as an example."

Zachary, looking extremely interested, places his hand to his chin, and slightly pushing Peter aside, steps forward to look at the bench. "Well, let me see that. My, that's a fine bit of craftsmanship, isn't it?" Running his hands over the bench, bending over, looking underneath, and walking around it. ''Oh yes, that is a fine piece of work. Don't happen to know who created it, do you, Paul?"

Paul looks down at the ground to somewhat hide his humor at Zachary's mirth. ''No, no, I don't, Zachary. Sorry."

Peter, now somewhat inspired by Zachary's exuberance over this simple bench, has been lured forward to study it more closely, along with Zachary. "Look over here, Pete. Look at the end. Look how this fellow has carved this. See the swirls? A really ornate, exceptional piece of work, wouldn't you say?"

Peter studies the scrollwork on the support and, looking up at Zachary, a bit bewildered at his enthusiasm answers, "Well, yes, it is." Getting caught up in the momentum of Zachary's enthusiasm, he begins to point out additional aspects of quality to Zachary. "Look here at the edges, the bevel is perfect! I mean, look at these lines. Who could do such a work?"

Paul has quietly risen and moved back a bit to give them both room to study the bench.

Equally silently has been the approach of the two female entities, the taller one still bearing the book under her arm. "Hello, fellows. What's up here today?"

Again startled by the sound of yet another voice, Peter jumps a bit, and turns, "Hello, there. Just... well, you know... looking at this bench. Really fine workmanship, " and he looks to Zachary for support.

Zachary nods at Peter and gives him a wink, "Oh, yes, this is a real fine bench. Not the ordinary kind you'd find. Look at this scroll work down here on the support."

As the group continues to study the bench, there is growing exuberance. Each time one of them expounds some admiration of the craftsmanship, it's as though a resonance occurs.

Finally, Zachary suggests, "Why don't we all seat ourselves on this fine bench and discuss this further?" and with a swift action, he slips over the top of the bench and seats himself.

Peter stands there a bit bewildered, pondering Zachary's manners. After all, there are ladies present, and Zachary has seated himself on the only bench.

Knowing Peter's thoughts, Zachary states, "Not a problem, Pete. They can sit on the other benches right there."

"Well, Zack, there is only this one... Where did those benches come from?" Looking up and down the pathway as far as Peter can see are replicas of this beautiful bench. Obviously in a state of some disbelief and bewilderment, his cloak begins to sparkle, almost audibly crackling, as he turns inwardly to balance himself.

Graciously, the others seat themselves and await Peter's return to a balanced state.

Zachary, with a demonstration of concern, jumps up and takes Peter by the arm, "Here... Sit down, Pete. Don't overload yourself over this. It's quite simple, you know."

Balanced and reassured by the touch of his friend, Peter asks, "What just happened here? How is it that these things keep happening here? What sort of a place is this, anyway? It just seems so strange and... well, overwhelming."

Paul gently answers, "What has been shown to you here, Peter, is intended only as a loving example, and is in no way meant to unbalance or unsettle you. If it has done so, please accept our most gracious apologies."

"Oh, yes, Pete," Zachary chimes in swiftly, "Didn't mean to jostle you with that, but it did get your attention, didn't it?"

Zachary's smile and knowing wink are all it takes to balance Peter again. He even manages to chuckle. As he does, he is aware of the occurrence of something he has noticed before... as though his laughter is like little rivulets of light cascading across all that is present. As he looks into the faces of his small group of friends, they are all warmly returning his gaze. "Could I change the subject just for a moment? What makes that dancing, light-like stuff I see once in a while? I saw it when we were at the field of flowers, when you all were laughing, and I saw it again, just now."

"He's right," agrees Zachary with enthusiasm. "I can vouch for it. I saw it, too."

With that, Peter and the others barely can constrain their humor, and as they do so, more of the lights appear and dance about. But this time, Peter not only sees them, but hears them as well. He hears the laughter resonating. "My goodness," he exclaims. "You can even *hear* the movement of the light, or whatever it is."

Zachary jumps in again. "He's right, again. I heard them, too, every bit as real as I hear myself speaking now."

Laughter now pours forth from everyone, and the atmosphere is filled with a collage of beautiful, symphonic, colored sound.

At this, Peter draws back in wonder, and as he does so, the others cease their laughter and calm themselves in respect for Peter.

Zachary puts his hand on Peter's shoulder, and, looking at him out of the corner of his eye, states, "This is a strange bunch you've got here, Pete, don't you think?"

This time, much more comfortable with this growing friendship, Peter uses Zachary's trademark of the knowing grin and says, "Okay, Zack, what are you up to now?"

Zachary withdraws his hand, and puts both hands into his lap and looks down, feigning some attitude of having been discovered… saying nothing but just looking down.

"That's just Zachary's way," Paul offers. "He's very unlimited and, therefore, doesn't tend to follow protocol much. Some might even say he leans a bit towards the impatient side at times, as well."

Paul looks at Zachary and Zachary looks at Paul, both grinning at one another. "You're right, Paul, absolutely right. I'm going to work on that. Seems I'm always taking these actions and then creating some sort of disturbance. I need to learn how to harmonize with things. Maybe we could all work together on that. Perhaps you could all help me to learn how to harmonize and blend in just a bit more. Would that be okay with all of you?" He suddenly turns to look squarely at Peter. "Would that be okay with you, Pete?"

Backing up a pace or two, Peter answers with a hint of uncertainty, "Well, sure, Zack. Anything to help."

With this, Zachary rather dramatically takes a posture as though he is about to utter forth an aria of operatic nature. Instead of the bombastic sound one might anticipate from his mirthfully grandiose gestures, an incredibly beautiful, soft, gentle sound comes forth from him.

Amazed by this expression of beautiful sound, Peter leans forward to see how it is being produced, since Zachary is turned so that Peter can't quite fully see his face. As Peter leans forward, Zachary gradually turns. The more Peter leans, the more Zachary turns, until Peter nearly falls off the bench. With this, the others again burst into laughter. Instantly, the sound, which appears to be coming from Zachary, is blended into a harmonic so grand and resonating that Peter feels the vibration all throughout his being. As he does, he feels vitalized, rejuvenated, as though he is actually being elevated or lifted up off the ground, and he loses himself in the wonder of the sound.

The next thing Peter is aware of is Paul's touch upon his arm. As though waking from a sleep, Peter looks into Paul's eyes. They are gently and lovingly reaching out to him in the same manner as his hand and arm are, and Peter thinks, *What is this? What has happened?*

Before Peter can vocalize those thoughts, Paul answers, "The resonance of sound, the influence of sound, goes well beyond that which you are accustomed to from your lifetime on Earth. Come. Sit down for a moment here by me, and we'll discuss it."

As Peter seats himself, he looks about. The females are quietly seated and Zachary is now back upon the bench, busily straightening out his spiritual cloak, acting nonchalant.

Paul compassionately places his arm about Peter, "You see, Peter, all things exist because of will. Will is that force which allows or creates in accordance with the force and the agreement of that which is the initiating force… that which has done the willing or the thinking.

"In the example of the purple flowers, of which you were the co-creator with God, you noted the essence of the flowers as though it were a living color. What you did not distinguish at that point was the resonance of that color expressed in another dimension, which you remember as sound. Yet, sound is much more than the simple undulation of Earth's atmosphere, or what you called sound waves. It is actually a creative force.

"Mind and spirit, when in harmony, can employ such forces for the creation of things. An example being the bench we were seated upon… while you did not discern it as also having properties of sound, when you touched the bench the second time, you did detect vibrational frequencies, sufficient enough that I knew you were capable of dealing with this next level of existence, which is defined here for you now, for your understanding, under the term 'sound.'

"Zachary was gracious enough to produce his own impromptu aria. In turn, we were inspired to join with him, rather inadvertently, and the resulting product you heard was the combination of our wills, our thought, as co-creators with God. Am I making myself clear to you, Peter?"

Peter has, to his own amazement, actually understood every word of what Paul has said. That he could comprehend this concept is of such wonder to him, he can't help but look to his colleagues. As he does, he notes that the auburn-haired entity is holding the book in front of her, resting it at an incline against her torso so that it is more or less facing him, as one would hold a mirror for another to look into it. Becoming much more alert now for such subtleties, due to his experiences to this point, Peter makes a mental note of this.

He next turns to Zachary, who is now inclined on the bench and is resting on one elbow, peering at him and fidgeting a bit with his cloak. When Peter's gaze falls on Zachary, Zachary responds with his whimsical grin and a broad wink.

Peter thinks to himself, *One just can't help but love that fellow.*

With this, Zachary nods just a bit, and Peter is embarrassed realizing that Zachary has perceived his thought.

Turning back to Paul, who is patiently awaiting Peter's next question, Peter asks, "Could I do that? I mean, just like Zachary did? On Earth I couldn't carry a tune. My wife used to say to me, 'Please, don't sing in the shower. The dog howls when you do, and the neighbors complain'."

They all laugh at this until Zachary stands and rather confidently walks up to Peter. "Not a problem. I can teach you. I've got an excellent voice, or so I'm told. Lots of friends often ask me over for sing-alongs."

Attempting to return Zachary's good-natured humor, Peter cocks his head and leans back grasping his knee, teasing, "Well, I'm not totally sure you're the one to coach me. You sounded a little flat towards the end of that aria. Perhaps it wouldn't hurt for you to practice a bit more."

Zachary leans in to Peter, "Absolutely right, my lad. How astute of you to catch that. You have a good ear there. All that time you spent listening to music on Earth didn't do you a bit of harm. No sir, not a bit of harm. I'll get to work on that. As a matter of fact, let's try a few bars right now. What do you say?"

Caught in the spirit of Zachary's humor and exuberance, Peter nods at Zachary. "You go ahead, Zack. I'll just listen and observe this first round, if you don't mind."

Needing no further invitation, Zachary again goes through his preparatory grandiose gestures, but this time he does so fully facing Peter. Outstretching an arm, as though he were reaching off into the distance or singing to something suspended in mid-air, Zachary creates a sound with no movement of his mouth. Sustaining the sound for a brief moment, he then brings his arm back down and looks at Peter, stating, "How was that? Better? The continuity of the tone, I thought, was particularly good."

Peter, now sitting erect and looking at Zachary, asks, "I didn't see your lips move. Nothing. I'm beginning to understand here. What you're showing me is that sound is not necessarily created in the same way I am used to. Is that it?" Zachary nods to Peter, and Peter goes on, taking this as an encouragement to do so. "Do you have a mechanism that you employ? You know, a procedure that I could follow so that I could do that?"

Peter continues to study Zachary, who looks as though he's thinking and trying to remember.

As Zachary continues to ponder, Paul answers for him, "Yes, I'm sure of it. Zachary can teach you. He knows a great deal about this sort of thing."

Zachary then, turning to Peter, states, "Do you think Paul is right, Pete? Do you think that I could teach you that?"

Peter sees that Paul is looking directly at him, smiling broadly, giving him a nod. Peter catches on. "Oh, yes, Zack, I'm sure of it. Go ahead."

Zachary dutifully answers, "Well, if you think I can, Pete, I'll give it a try. Come and stand by me, then, shoulder to shoulder here, and look up at that spot that I was pointing to up there."

Looking upwards, Peter strains to perceive something,

but seeing nothing, turns to him and says, "I'm looking, Zack, but I don't see anything."

"Keep watching. Just keep watching. And try to think and remember the sound you heard. Now, close your eyes a moment and clear your mind and just relax, and try again to remember the sound."

Peter closes his eyes. Almost instantly, the sound is there, resonating so clearly and brilliantly all through his body, that it causes him to abruptly open his eyes.

Zachary is still pointing at the spot, and as Peter's eyes move to it, he sees a brilliant orb of golden yellow. So beautiful and so brilliant is the color that Peter's concentration is broken, and the sound stops. As it does, the color takes form and flutters down. Resting on Zachary's up-stretched hand is a beautiful golden butterfly.

In wonder, Peter studies the creature now perched atop the end of Zachary's index finger.

Zachary slowly brings it down close to his own eyes and states quietly, "Well, good day, there. How very lovely you are. It is wonderful to have you with us today."

Peter, watching, mouth agape, turns to look at Paul, who is still seated. With another smile, Paul nods at Peter, pointing to the bench.

Zachary steps over to the other bench, still talking to the butterfly, which seems to be leaving a trail of golden-yellow light, as Zachary walks.

"That was an interesting experiment, wasn't it, Peter?" Paul asks.

Peter reorganizes his thoughts for a few moments, sparkling as he does, and answers, "It certainly was," turning his head moment to moment, to see if the butterfly is still there or if it is going to vanish like the purple flowers did.

"Would you like to know more about that?"

"I sure would, Paul. What happened? I couldn't believe it when I opened my eyes, it seemed as though the sound was coming from me. Yet I wasn't singing."

"You weren't singing as you knew it on Earth. You were thinking. Those sounds were from your thought."

"They were?" asks Peter excitedly. "Really?"

"That's right," continues Paul, "and furthermore, the creation of the light and that butterfly over there are products of your doing."

Incredulously, Peter looks from Paul's gentle, honest, loving eyes to the butterfly, which Zachary is still speaking to softly. Turning back to Paul, Peter asks, "You mean I actually created that butterfly? I wasn't thinking of a butterfly. How did I create a butterfly?"

"It wasn't so much that you 'created' the butterfly," Paul answers. "You created the 'opportunity' for creation. And since you were fond of such creatures on Earth, this symbolically, then, represents something of your own nature, your own fondness. When you opened yourself, you came forth in the form of something pleasurable from within your being... one of your joys. See what I mean?"

Turning again, Peter notes that Zachary is now standing in front of him, his hand outstretched with the butterfly still on the tip of one finger. "Thanks for letting me chat with him... a lovely creature. You can have him back now. I have an appointment to keep."

Without waiting for a response from anyone, Zachary turns and begins to stride away. Then, calling back over his shoulder, "Thanks for the grand afternoon, Pete. We'll have to sing again soon."

Peter, now holding this brilliant orb of golden yellow light in the form of a butterfly, notes with wonder the power that is seemingly now available to him. Continued discussion about this with his colleagues lies ahead, but as you consider whether or not this is indeed a possibility, remember this:

"So as man does believe and thinketh in his heart, so is he."

Dependent upon your belief and your faith, so is your position as a co-creator with God assured.

CHAPTER 5

The Crystal Workers' Realm
JUNE 4, 1990

We would preface this chapter with these comments:
Firstly, that it is the intent of these works to provide
an illumination to your pathway that will promote under-
standing regarding what lies beyond this incarnation, and
make the way just that much more passable for you as you
move beyond this incarnation into other realms.

We pray as well that the meaning and content might
be a form of understanding with which you can meet and deal
with each event or circumstance. That is and shall ever be
our prayer henceforth.

P eter is seated now with his friend and companion, Paul,
approximately where we had left them previously, with
Peter having this brilliant-colored butterfly perched
upon the tip of his finger.

"Are you saying, Paul, that somehow or other,
through my own thought or mind, even unknowingly, I have
created this?" looking at the butterfly

Nodding, Paul answers, "Yes, absolutely."

Peter is studying the butterfly, "What sort of a
creature is this, actually? Comparatively speaking now, Paul,
I've seen lots of butterflies at my study window. In fact, as
you may know, I had many flowers planted there just because
I enjoyed seeing them and the hummingbirds and other
insects working busily while I was in my study."

"You are correct. I did know that."

Glancing at Paul, "So is it that, because I had a

fascination and fondness for the butterflies in my flower garden, somehow or other the sound I created simply by thinking of it ended up by creating this beautiful creature?"

Again, Paul nods. "Yes, that is so."

"Well, I'd like to ask you now about two hundred questions all at once."

"I understand completely," chuckles Paul, "and I'll do the best I can to answer."

At that moment, a jingling sound gradually begins to grow stronger and stronger until it is quite loud. Peter straightens up, looks about, and as he does he can see the top of Zachary's head bobbing up and down as he comes up the little knoll along the pathway to where they are seated. Jingle-jingle. Jingle, jingle, jingle.

Zachary, seeing Peter's gaze, waves vigorously, a large smile on his face, calling, "See? I promised I'd announce the next time I was coming. How was that?"

Peter, amused, exuberantly rises to greet Zachary.

Paul, also amused, adds, "You can turn it off now, Zachary. It's getting a little loud, don't you think?"

Obediently, the sound instantly stops, and Zachary comes to rest on the bench across from Peter and Paul. "Still have your friend there, I see."

"Yes, I do."

"Like him, do you?"

"Well, yes. He is so beautiful."

"Couldn't agree more, Pete. One of the best I've seen. Of course, I'd prefer a different color were it mine, but beautiful, nonetheless."

Peter, silently amused, simply nods at Zachary, still fascinated with the butterfly.

Without pausing a moment, Zachary continues, "I have a bit of a journey to take and just thought I'd stop by to see if you two, or... if you're busy, Paul, if Pete, here, would like to join me."

A sense of anticipation passes through Peter, indicated by a rather crackling staccato of white light dancing about on his cloak.

Paul turns to Peter calmly and states, "Well, it's quite all right with me, Peter, if it's okay with you. We can always continue our discussion at some other point."

Peter, sensing just a bit of apprehension rising within him, asks in a small voice, "Where is it you're going, Zack?"

"Well, I have to go to another place. Need to do a bit of work there. Shouldn't be too long. Nice chaps in that locale. You might find it interesting, especially in view of your recent accomplishments. These folks do a lot of work with that sort of thing where they are."

"Just exactly where are they, anyway, Zack? Is it a long journey?" Peter inquires, still apprehensive as it suddenly dawns on him that he has not thought of there being any place other than where he is at the moment. Not that there couldn't be. He simply hasn't thought of it, perhaps because the others have kept him too preoccupied to think about anything else other than what has been happening.

Knowing this thought of Peter's, Paul answers, "There are actually many other places we could go, Peter, and many other entities that we could meet. It is up to you. Zachary is well-known and well-liked in those realms, and is a good traveling companion, but the decision is yours."

Remembering his manners, Peter turns to Zachary and asks, "We wouldn't be in the way, would we?"

Zachary robustly jumps to his feet and states, "Oh, of course not. You'd be a welcome addition to my journey. Sometimes it gets very boring without a friend to talk with. Joy is very limited when there's no one to share it with. Don't you think?"

"Well, yes, I guess so. I hadn't really thought about it recently, but I do have more fun when I'm with you," realizing in that moment that he hasn't been without one or more of them since he arrived.

"Well, then… let's get about our preparations."

Paul stands and joins Zachary and reaches a hand to Peter. "Ready?"

Peter, feeling twinges of uneasiness and anticipation, rises and, looking at the butterfly and then back at Paul, asks, "What about him, Paul?"

"Take him along, if you wish, or simply place him on those flowers over there and we can get him when we return."

Pausing a moment, Peter reaches his hand out, and the butterfly delicately flutters to a nearby flower and perches there, adding luster to the flower's already brilliant colors and fragrance.

"He'll be just fine, Pete," Zachary offers reassuringly. "Shall we?"

With that, Paul and Zachary each take one of Peter's arms and they begin to move off down the pathway. As they do, Peter feels a strange sensation coming over him.

"Feeling all right?" Paul asks.

"Yes, I… I think so."

"Zachary," offers Paul, "shall we give him one of our cloaks. He might travel better with it, don't you think?"

"Oh, yes, terribly thoughtless of me. Just a moment… I have a spare right here," with which he reaches behind and pulls forth a lovely, radiant blue-white garment, and, as he unfolds it, it gives off a hint of a melodious sound. In a swift motion, Zachary embraces Peter's entire being with this cloak.

"Say, that does feel good, Zack. Thank you. What a marvelous feeling this has. I feel very warm and comfortable and at peace. A bit weary, though. Strange, I haven't felt this way the entire time I've been here. Except for that time when we got to the end of those colors. I must have rested a long time there."

"Not at all," Paul comments, further reassuring Peter.

"It is good for one to have some balancing time occasionally, or sleep, as you call it. If you would like to rest for a short while, feel free to do so. In fact," pointing over to the side, "Zachary appears to be ready for one, too."

Zachary has taken a position on a lush expanse of green grass dotted with brilliant little flowers that electrify the greenness with the contrast of their colors and hues.

"Gosh, this is soft. Come and join me, fellows," Zachary calls. "Time for a break, don't you think?"

In a few moments, Peter passes easily into a period of rest. Paul and Zachary align themselves on each side of him and shift into their own state of balance as they await his return to consciousness.

An indeterminable amount of time later, Peter opens his eyes, immediately noting a difference. Quickly, he turns to look for his friends and sees Paul to his right and Zachary to his left, apparently occupied with some discussion.

They turn simultaneously to look at Peter and smile.

"Feeling better?" Zachary asks.

"Why yes, indeed, I feel very good. Thank you." Looking to Paul, "Was I gone long?"

"It wasn't long at all, Peter, and, at any rate, it wouldn't matter," he offers gently.

Zachary reaches down and brushes off his cloak, commenting casually, "This stuff sure seems to stick on here. Let me take a look at yours, Pete." He turns Peter about, making motions as if brushing something off. "Is that better?"

"Why, yes, Zack, I feel terrific. Thanks for your concern. This cloak you've given me is particularly special in some way. Really makes me feel at ease... comfortable."

"That's great, Pete, just what I wanted to hear. Wouldn't want to give you a shoddy cloak, you know. A person's got to remember his reputation. Things like this get around." With that, he chuckles lightly, reciprocated by Paul, who is observing all this.

"He looks good to me, Zachary. You have done well, as usual. I particularly like that cloak."

"Good. Good. Made it myself," Zachary answers, casting a wink at Peter.

Peter could not know how much truth there is in what Zachary has just stated. For, to further explain the properties of the cloak, beyond that which has been given previously, it is, in essence, the literal expression of Zachary's spirituality, and an extension of his love for Peter. As he embraced Peter with it and then activated it with what Peter thought was simply Zachary brushing off debris, Zachary has insured Peter's preservation beyond any measure. Paradoxically, in addition, he has taken measures to prevent Peter's presence from infringing upon any other souls Peter may encounter in this new realm.

For your reference, this realm they are now in is much closer to the Earth, in comparison to the Garden Realm. The souls in this realm, although they are not what might be considered earthbound, are souls who are very much involved with the Earth and will probably reincarnate there again. In fact, it is likely that they will do so more than once. These souls are thought of as benevolent souls, in no way harmful or of malicious intent. To the contrary, it is their love and their intention of doing good works – albeit obsessive – that, curiously, has bound them to the Earth. They do not know they are bound, however, for they know not that which is beyond their realm.

Emerging from a cloud-like mist, Peter, still between Zachary and Paul, begins to observe their surroundings. Immediately he notes there seems to be a lack here of color. The colors, while they are present, do not seem to have the vibrancy, the luster as they do in his Garden Ream. The hues are merely different shades, and do not have the life or light.

Looking down at the path they are following, he notes it is uneven, irregular, and that there are pebbles of such different sizes that could be obstacles if one weren't careful. The edge of the grass, which comes up to the path, is irregular. Looking about the grass for the delightful little flowers he is now familiar with, he sees that, while there are a few here and there, they do not have the brilliance of contrast, the luminosity he has come to love. Even the sky above him, while displaying varying hues, and including some which are brighter than others, most are very dull. In general, the vibrancy of this realm seems to be considerably less than that which he had observed in his garden.

Paul and Zachary seem intent upon their movement, looking off to the side here and there and continuing to move steadily forward. Peter feels for some reason as though he should not speak, and rather dutifully follows between them.

Ahead just a bit, Peter begins to make out the angular shape of a structure. This piques his interest greatly, for he hasn't seen buildings since he has moved into these realms, or at least, if he has, does not remember them.

Without taking his eyes off the structure, he leans towards the left where Zachary is and asks quietly, "Zack, that looks like a building up there. Where are we, anyway?"

Zachary, imitating Peter, leans his head and, continuing to look straight ahead, whispers, "I think you're right. That does look like a building. Strange, isn't it?"

Peter answers in the same mannerism as before, "Yes, it is. What do they need a building for, anyway?"

"Beats me. Maybe it's just what they're used to."

Peter can hear Paul chuckling softly at their conversation, and as they continue to move, Peter reflects upon his own words, wondering why he said what he did. *So much has happened,* he thinks to himself, *I never realized we didn't have buildings or houses in the Garden. I haven't heard of any adverse weather or anything. Maybe the Garden Realm has a different climate than there is here.*

Zachary leans over, again imitating Peter's earlier

mannerism, still staring straight ahead and in a half-whisper answers Peter's unspoken thoughts, "Maybe it rains here, or something like that. Who knows?"

Peter nods an affirmation without thinking, and, continuing to whisper, says, "Yes... maybe that's it."

As they approach the apparent entrance to the structure, Peter studies it carefully, marveling at how well constructed it appears. It looks to him that it was very carefully done, no indication of any shoddiness of workmanship. The structure seems to be seamless, as though it were created in some way all from one piece of something.

"Marvelous finishing work," he whispers to Zachary.

"Indeed so. Must have taken quite a while to build," whispers Zachary.

Peter is considering Zachary's last comment as they enter what looks like a hallway or corridor leading into a large chamber. Quickly surveying the chamber, Peter sees that there is a line of bookcases, and numerous tables, chairs, and apparati of various types throughout the very large hall.

He then notes the presence of entities, and gasps in reaction to what he perceives... these entities all have on dull garments, they lack luster. There are some patches of very brilliant color, but for the most part they are out of hue, almost as though they clash. Some are mottled. Some are more consistently one color, but the color is very dull. Others have colors in them that seem to run angularly in jagged, serrated patterns, intertwining with others. He notices that the entities are busy, studying and working on something.

Paul turns to Peter. "Are you doing well? Do you need anything?"

"No, thank you, but I must say... this place is very different from the Garden, isn't it?"

"Yes, indeed it is," Paul answers. "Perhaps it is good that Zachary invited us along, so that you could see these differences."

"Wouldn't have thought to make the journey without you," Zachary adds. "Would have missed your companionship. But now, if you'll excuse me, I've got some work to do here. One needs to be mindful of who one is working for, you know." With that, he turns about and swiftly strides across the room.

Peter's eyes follow him carefully as he heads towards an entity at a corner table. Peter feels a sense of apprehension, and a feeling of fondness sweeps over him as he watches his friend leave.

As Peter's eyes continue to be riveted on Zachary, he feels a touch on his right shoulder. "He'll be just fine, Peter."

Turning to Paul, who has always been understanding and informative, Peter blurts out a torrent of questions. "What is happening with me, Paul? I had forgotten how it felt to experience what I'm feeling now. These are like emotions I felt on Earth. For an instant there, it was as though I was feeling what I remember as remorse or sadness at the loss of someone. I know that is not the case here. I mean, Zachary is coming back, isn't he?" he asks with a bit of anxiety.

Paul smiles warmly at Peter, "Zachary is your friend, Peter. He would never leave you... you can depend on that."

Obviously relieved by that statement, Peter now returns to his observation of the surroundings. He notices that many of the entities are working on something that looks like pieces of glass.

Paul explains, "Those are crystals. Remember them? You have them on Earth."

"Oh, sure. We had some once in a home that I was growing up in. They were hanging from the ceiling, of all places. As a child I used to like to look at them. They were part of a big chandelier. Ever seen one of those, Paul?"

"I know what you mean, I can see it in your thought."

"You can?" he asks, incredulously.

"Certainly. Thought is alive, Peter, a living thing. And

because of our friendship and our bond, as you might call it, we have nothing separating us from each other. Therefore, what is visible in your mind I can perceive, and what is visible in mine you can perceive… that is, if you wish or have a need to."

This thought causes Peter to step within himself and he begins to sparkle again. Immediately, Paul reaches out and touches Peter on the shoulder, and the sparkling instantly stops. Peter looks about the room and notices that several of the individuals who had been working are now looking up in his direction. Zachary, over in a comer, has turned to look back at Peter. Embarrassed that he may have caused a disturbance, Peter whispers to Paul, "Sorry about that."

Paul smiles and nods, "Not a problem. They didn't actually see that. They just intuited it."

"What do you mean, they didn't see it? How could they not see it? It makes quite a racket when it happens."

Paul turns to Peter again, "Peter, I'm going to tell you some things now that may be difficult for you to comprehend completely. So, try to keep your mind open and not let your reason or logic get in the way. Just let the information come into your mind as I'm offering it to you, and I will try to impart this understanding. Is that acceptable?"

Looking into the eyes of his friend, who at this point has a hand on each shoulder and is facing him squarely, Peter can accept this, for he can see within Paul an attitude of love and kindness and truth which would dispel any doubt that he might have had. "Sure, Paul. Go ahead."

With this, Paul begins to speak more and more softly, until Peter can barely make out what he is saying. The more Paul speaks, the softer the words become, until Peter finds himself actually straining to hear.

As he does, something strange happens. It is as though someone quickly, swiftly, turns the volume of a receiving device way up. Paul's voice is now clear and melodious inside him, and seems to resonate in a unique and new way. Curiously, Peter is understanding all that Paul is saying to him, and is even able to visualize and comprehend all the nuances and inflections Paul is giving him.

Then just as swiftly, it stops, at which point Peter blinks, as though he has been daydreaming for a moment, and he realizes that Paul has taken his hands off his shoulders and is standing before him, studying him.

"Gosh, Paul, that was remarkable. I understood everything you were saying. I'm glad you spoke up, though. I missed the first part."

Smiling at Peter, Paul responds, "I neither spoke softly nor loudly."

"Well, I don't know what was wrong, then. Maybe it's this cloak I have on that Zack gave me, or something, but I couldn't hear you at first."

Paul, again looking very directly at Peter answers, "You didn't hear me at all, Peter. You were aware of my thoughts. That's what you experienced. You weren't hearing with ears... you were knowing. We were communicating with thought."

In wonder, Peter responds, "Truly? I mean, are you saying that I was hearing your thoughts? No wonder I could see all those pictures you were describing so clearly. That's amazing. What turns that sort of thing on and off?"

"Need, desire, or willingness. They are the keys."

"Wow! How I could have used that on Earth."

Paul chuckles a bit. "You did, Peter... more than you realize. Most do, and don't realize it until much later." With that, he gently takes Peter's elbow, guiding him over to a table where an elderly-looking man is diligently working.

"This man is working with a thought," explains Paul quietly. "He is trying to create a thought-form that will be helpful to people on Earth. As he does, he is fashioning it in the form here before you, of what you've called a crystal.

Like that chandelier you showed me."

Gazing at the elderly man and the crystal, Peter whispers to Paul, "He doesn't seem to be bothered by our presence. He must be really concentrating hard."

"He is concentrating hard, that is true. But the reason he is not bothered by our presence is because he cannot see us. We are not visible to him in this realm."

"Just what do you mean by that, Paul? Why can't he see us, when we can see him?"

"Well, that could be a long explanation, and we'll get into it. But perhaps it would be sufficient now for you to know that those who are of a higher vibration or frequency are not perceptible to those in lower frequencies; and we have, in a way, moved downward from the Garden Realm. We can, however, make it possible for these entities to see us, as Zachary has done over there, simply by adjusting our cloaks."

Peter contemplates what Paul has told him, then turns to the entity before them again. "So what does the crystal have to do with the thought-form the man is attempting to build? How does one build a thought-form, anyway? He looks like he's doing a lot of labor, but yet I don't see what it is he's laboring over, other than the crystal in front of him and lots of notes and stuff. How does he get the thought-form into that crystal, if in fact that's what he's doing? Why is he doing that, and what is he going to do with the crystal when he's finished?"

"You've given me a number of questions, there," chuckles Paul. "Zachary seems to be able to answer those kinds of questions easier than I—than most, in fact, but I'll do the best I can. These are very good questions, though, Peter, and I will also learn as I attempt to answer them for you.

"You see, in this realm there are entities who are truly loving souls. But through the intensity of their love, they have, in some cases inadvertently (and in other cases through their own choice) formed a bond of sorts to the Earth, or to another realm adjacent to the Earth.

"That bond is somewhat like what you would envision as a tether, which is preventing them from reaching the full measure of their own awareness. In other words, these entities believe that they must be here because this is the highest realm they can perceive. They don't believe that there are other realms beyond this. They believe that this is it… that this is where you go when you leave the Earth. And that is so for them, until they can release those bonds. The thought-form he's attempting to build is much like the thought he was trying to build on Earth.

"This particular entity was a teacher, a very dedicated, loving, and well-loved person. He was seriously concerned about the intelligence and the preparedness of those who were his students, and he did his very best to give them a concept not only of knowledge, but also of the appropriateness of living life. He taught them of certain conditions which he considered in that time to be the hallmarks or foundational stones of proper living. You might recognize some of them such as cleanliness, proper diet, an attentiveness to schedule and to work habits, having directions and goals, and a firm and deliberate practice and belief in God.

"The thought-form he's attempting to construct now is really not much different than this, for he believes it is correct. He is fashioning this thought-form through a mechanism he has discovered which enables him to continue to help others on Earth. It is a means by which he can continue to do what he believes he must, and what he believes is his chosen work, or purpose, under the guidance of God.

"He uses the crystal you see in front of him as a symbol, as a focal point to help him concentrate. He has learned that he can fashion a limited form of thought, which can transcend the veils which separate these realms from the Earth. He is attempting to develop it to the point where it has sufficient quality to penetrate those veils and reach the Earth in answer to prayers which he has heard and seen from there.

"Those prayers reach him here, in accordance with his will to be of service to God. You see... the entire matter is truly admirable. The intent is pure. But the limited sight and understanding prevents him from functioning to the fullness of his capacity, and from doing much more than he is presently doing. Did that help to answer your questions?"

Peter, studying Paul and contemplating what he has just given, looks from Paul down to the little man and back again. "Of course you know I have lots of questions about all of this, but let me ask you this first... why is it that this man and some of the other people here so ...well, I don't know... old or something?"

Paul smiles at Peter's blunt question. "Because that is what they are. Their ideas are old. Their thought-forms are old. Their limitations are old. So all that is within them is what you perceive outwardly."

"All that is within them is what I perceive outwardly. Is that what you said?"

Paul nods at Peter.

Peter then turns to look again at the old man before him and then at the others around the room. *They all have the same appearance and feel the same,* he thinks to himself. *In fact, this room, in all its dullness, feels like them.*

In that moment Peter recognizes Zachary's familiar tinkling sound. Looking towards where Zachary is standing, he sees Zachary motioning him to come over. Peter looks to Paul, who nods reassuringly, and Peter walks cautiously towards Zachary, with Paul following immediately behind.

"I'd like you to meet a fellow here, Pete, so let's make an adjustment to your cloak so he can see you. This fellow's quite a good man. He's made lots of progress recently.

"Wilbur, this is Peter, my old friend. We've been together a long time."

Peter looks as though he's about to question what Zachary means by this, when Wilbur stands and bows courteously. With a broad smile, looking back and forth from Peter to Zachary, he extends a hand to Peter.

Abruptly, Paul steps between Wilbur and Peter and says, "Excuse me, Zachary, but we need to be going now."

Peter looks questioningly at Paul, and with an awkward smile at Wilbur, who has quickly stepped aside.

"Now, Wilbur," Zachary says, "if you need anything, just call on Peter and he'll give you a hand."

Peter is incredulous as he hears what Zachary has just said, while Wilbur is looking back and forth from Zachary to Peter, nodding, obviously pleased.

With that, Zachary pats Wilbur on the shoulder, and Wilbur gives a bit of a bow to Peter, which seems formal, but nonetheless, Peter reciprocates.

Swiftly now, Zachary grasps one of Peter's arms and Paul the other, and they quickly move down to the corridor, outside of the structure, and back along the pathway.

"Hey, wait a minute, guys. What's going on here? Could we just stop a moment and talk about all this?"

"Oh, sure, Pete, but what do you say we go somewhere else first? There's not enough color here for me. I need that color. Gosh, I guess I've become more attached to it than I realized. Could we wait until we get home?"

Realizing he has not been given much leeway by Zachary, Peter responds uncertainly, "Oh... uh... sure thing, Zack," he answers. "Is this the way?"

With a glance over his shoulder, Zachary grins. "Well, it's *a* way... let's put it like that." With that, Zachary moves swiftly and steps in front of Peter, and with Paul falling in behind, they move ahead single-file.

In a moment, a wisp of cloud-like substance envelops them, and Peter slows his movement, looking about in wonder. Paul taps him gently on the shoulder, "Nothing to be concerned about, Peter. Just keep following Zachary."

Zachary, who is now in front and enveloped in this mist, appears as a beacon in the cloud, for his cloak has taken on a brilliant, blue-white, crystalline luminosity.

Seeing this, Peter looks down and observes that his own cloak is now the identical color. Casting a glance backwards, he sees that Paul's cloak is also the same. Then returning his gaze forward, he sees the cloud-like mist part, and as he looks down upon the pathway, he recognizes it to be a path in his Garden.

Having moved to their familiar knoll, Zachary collapses onto the grass and rolls over onto one side. Propping his head up with an elbow on the ground and touching one of the delicate flowers with his fingertips, he looks at Peter, "Now, what was it you were asking, Pete?"

Paul takes a cross-legged position a few feet from Zachary, and Peter seats himself across from them both.

"Well, I don't really know where to begin."

"Begin wherever you are," Zachary says nonchalantly. "We'll go backwards or forwards with what you want to know. Or, whatever... doesn't really matter."

"Okay, who is Wilbur, and why in the world did you tell him that if he needs anything to ask me? I've never seen him before. And what would he ask me for, anyway? I don't know anything."

Zachary straightens himself up and asks, "Now, why would you make a statement like that? After all, you've got that book and everything and those ladies to help you, too. Then there's Paul over there. And me, too. So what more could you ask for?"

Disarmed, Peter stammers, "W-well, what do you mean? All these things you claim that I have... what am I to do with them? How can I help this Wilbur? I mean, what kind of help is it that he needs, anyway?"

Zachary grins a bit as he answers, "How should I

know what kind of help he needs? That's your job, not mine. Goodness knows I have enough to do."

Paul chuckles at Zachary, and rocks back and forth.

At that moment, Peter realizes the two female entities have joined them and are standing just a few feet away.

Zachary motions to them. "Come join us. We've had a wonderful outing, and Peter wants to tell you about it. He's even made a new friend. Gosh, he's getting more and more popular all the time."

Paul is continuing to laugh, nearly to the point of tearfulness. Peter can't help himself and joins in with Paul. Paul calms himself and offers, "You must forgive Zachary, Peter. He's a great fellow, but he is given to jest... a bit more than is appropriate perhaps. I'm not judging him, mind you. I enjoy it. It's just an observation, and I thought it would be well for me to point out to you that he is jesting, and he's trying to point something out to you at the same time."

With a bit more seriousness now, Zachary responds to Paul's opening in this way, "Every entity, Peter, has certain focal points that are of importance to them. Right?"

"Well, I guess so."

"What do you mean, you guess so? After all, you've got that butterfly of yours sitting there on your shoulder."

Peter quickly looks to the shoulder Zachary has indicated and discovers that the butterfly has returned and is, indeed, perched there.

"So you see," continues Zachary off-handedly, "if there are certain things that you are clinging to, why can't others cling to things? Like Wilbur, for example."

"Well, wait a minute, now, Zack," responds Peter. "I never said Wilbur was clinging to anything, and I'm not really clinging to this butterfly, either. I mean, I like it and all, but it's not an obsession with me."

"Oh. Well, that's good," answers Zachary, "because sometimes when one is obsessed with things, it has a way of making them poor conversationalists. They keep coming back to the same thing, over and over, and they keep repeating themselves. Have you ever noticed that, Paul?"

Feigning surprise at being called upon, Paul answers, "What? Who, me?"

"Yes, you," laughs Zachary.

Straightening himself, Paul responds, "Well, yes, as a matter of fact, I have noticed it. Particularly in realms like we just came from."

"Speaking of the realm we just came from," says Peter, "let me change topic here for a moment. Paul told me that this man we were watching was making a thought-form... that he had a crystal and was using it somehow. What was he going to do, anyway? Send it to the Earth somehow?"

"No, Pete," Zachary answers. "Not literally. We don't do that here. But, in effect, what he was intending to do was to use a common medium of exchange. In other words, you may recall that on Earth every person has certain things, focal points... objects which can become obsessions... not including butterflies, of course," he chuckles. "But, to the extent that a person has a focal point, then that focal point creates what you might think of as an opening, or a portal, through which varying forms of communication, or transmission of consciousness, can be accomplished."

"What exactly do you mean by 'forms of communication'?" asks Peter.

"Quite simply this... On Earth, there are many forms of symbolism, elements which can represent varying intents and have meaning which is of significance. To the extent they are believed in, they are imparted a certain degree of power or potential. Some of these have, as their native characteristic, certain tendencies which enable them to be capable of amplifying or converting some of the thought or intent. The more they are employed, the greater becomes their potential... not in and of themselves, but as an extension or a tool of the person using them.

"There are many variations of such symbols, or expressions. Some function better than others, and some are a focal point of group concentration, which amplifies them that much more. Others have a characteristic which you might find particularly interesting, and that is one which comes to them as the result of previous use, meaning the use of those elements or symbols in earlier activities of entities who lived before the current ones. Understand?" asks Zachary.

Sifting through the array of thoughts and words just given, Peter simply nods an affirmation.

"Very good. Since you understand, then I'll continue."

This causes Peter's eyebrows to rise considerably, and he makes a mental note that he won't simply affirm in the future, if he doesn't really understand.

Without hesitation, Zachary continues. "There are people on Earth for whom the relationship between these common focal points is an important one. In the essence of the crystal are certain properties, which I spoke of just above... and which you indicated you understood, and so... as these properties are seen to be good and purposeful, they are useful in multiple realms.

"The entities in the realm in which we just visited... you know, the one where your friend Wilbur lives..." (Zachary doesn't pause long enough to let Peter object to that) "...these entities are using the crystal as a means of contributing to the Earth. They're very strongly interested in continuing to contribute and to be a helpmeet to the needs of entities there. The more a freewill thought and intent is given – for example a prayer – the greater can be the amplification, and thus, the strength of that prayer. And they aren't the only ones. There are many other realms, and there are entities from some of them who also use such focal points, or openings, as an opportunity to work with, and on behalf of, other good works for any person striving for growth. Got all that?"

The pause is prolonged and intentional, for obviously Peter couldn't possibly have understood all of it, and Zachary knows that; what Zachary has offered Peter is sufficient for Peter to reflect upon for quite some time.

Zachary rises and, as is his habit, methodically begins to straighten his cloak and brush it off. "By the way, Pete, you can keep my cloak as long as you'd like," at which point Peter embarrassingly realizes that he still has it on. "No, no, don't get up. I've got a couple of errands to run," Zachary states, smiling broadly. "So you folks carry on here." And turning to Peter again, "Think about what we've talked about. And, uh... let me know if you need any help with Wilbur. Nice chap, that one. Shows lots of promise. See you soon." Before Peter can object, Zachary turns and strides off.

As Peter watches him walk away, Zachary, without turning, raises his hand. He makes a swirling motion, and his tinkling-jingling sound is heard again. He takes a few more steps and turns back with a wide grin, "Thought I'd better let you know when I was leaving, too," and with a wave, Zachary disappears over the knoll.

Peter turns to look at Paul whose eyes are warmly and compassionately studying him. "Are you doing well, Peter? Need a rest or anything?"

"I think I might fairly soon, Paul. This has been quite an experience. It's not that I actually feel tired, but taking those breaks as we've done seems to help me balance. I seem to be able to understand things better when I'm resting like that. Reminds me of those times in my study. But I guess you know about those, too."

Paul simply smiles. "Well, why don't you take your rest, and when you are ready, we'll go into this in any detail you would like. But just remember for now... there isn't anything that you need to do, or must do. Do whatever brings you joy. And that includes Wilbur. Zachary is a good friend of yours and is very fond of you. He would never want you to do anything that does not feel good to you. Do you know that?

"I do, Paul, and I've grown fond of him, too."

Mind and emotion do not terminate with the departure from Earth. Beyond the Earth, emotion is every bit as wonderful and as joyful as you experience it, and even greater, for emotion does not have to be manipulated, constrained, nor directed in accordance with what's expected of you. Your thoughts and emotions manifest themselves, whether that be in the form of a butterfly or a beautiful garden.

Such power to manifest awaits you, ever awaiting your claiming of it.

CHAPTER 6

Understanding the Cloak
AUGUST 7, 1990

As Peter learns more about "the cloak" and how it functions, so can you gain greater understanding of such a potential for you on Earth.

We now find Paul seated beside Peter, who has just awakened from a period of spiritual rest, or balance.

Peter props himself up. "Have I been away long?"

"As is always the case, Peter, that is of no concern. Are you well?"

"Indeed, I feel quite revitalized. These periods of rest are remarkable. They seem to do something that makes me feel almost electrified, as though I am so very alive. More than I could ever express to you, Paul."

Smiling, Paul nods and comments softly, "I understand completely. I feel the same."

Rising, they move the short distance to the bench, which was of such interest to Peter, and seat themselves. Paul turns to Peter and asks, "Are there any areas that you would like to discuss now, Peter? It appears we have the Garden Realm to ourselves for a time, and so whatever thoughts you might have or questions that are within you, I would welcome the opportunity of discussing them with you."

Peter, rather self-consciously, looks down and so doing, realizes he is still wearing the cloak given to him by Zachary. "Well, could we talk about this cloak that Zachary gave me?"

"Of course. What would you wish to know about it?"

"Well, there are so many things, though nothing really big." After a pause for reflection, "But like, what is it about this cloak that makes me feel so good? If I remove it, can I place it back on myself again? And what would have been the difference had I not had this on when we were visiting Wilbur... my new friend, as Zachary called him?"

"The cloak is more than a literal one of the kind your memory might recall to you from the Earth. It is a cloak of spirituality. It is the symbolic achievement of Zachary's spiritual awareness. Therefore, when you are wearing it, it has similar capabilities for you as it does for Zachary."

"Forgive me for interrupting, but what do you mean by 'similar capabilities'? What capability does Zachary have, anyway? Is this some sort of magical garment?"

"Since the cloak is the equivalent of Zachary's spiritual consciousness, it has the potential of enabling you, the wearer, to function in capacities similar to, if not nearly equal to, Zachary himself. Some might interpret that as having magical qualities or properties, but they aren't actually magical. They are quite logical, and they are ordered and structured in accordance with what we here call God's Law, or Universal Law... which is a topic, I have no doubt, we will enter into in considerable depths in times ahead.

"The cloak can be removed by you or by Zachary, and it can be, in a manner of speaking, re-installed. It is better for Zachary to actually do this initially, for reasons which are a bit complex. But look at it this way... it is Zachary's cloak and it is his gift to you. It would be an honor to him if you would allow him to assist you with it. However, there would be no harm in taking a moment to become more familiar with it. Would you care to remove it at this time?"

Somewhat apprehensive of Paul's suggestion, Peter pauses, and there is the crackling, popping sound and dancing lights that traditionally appear when Peter turns inward. They are subtle though, the reason being that Peter has considerable faith in Paul and since Paul made the suggestion, Peter is confident that all is aright.

"Very well." Standing, he looks at the cloak, then at Paul, and takes on a puzzled countenance. Again, he looks down and back and forth from the cloak to Paul.

Stifling a bit of a chuckle, Paul asks, "What is troubling you, Peter?"

"Well, Paul... uh... how do I take this off? I don't see any buttons or zippers or snaps or fasteners of any sort. Now that I really look at it, it appears to be one continuous piece of fabric, or... whatever this is. How would I remove it?"

Paul rises and faces Peter. "Quite simply. One would remove it first by will, and secondly by action."

Peter is studying Paul's face, allowing his words to permeate his consciousness. He thinks to himself, *first by will and then by action?*

Paul answers Peter's thought, "Yes, first by will. Will the cloak to be removed. It is as straightforward as that."

Focusing upon this as a concept, Peter adopts the techniques as guided earlier by Zachary... closes his eyes and instantly achieves a state of tranquility, as though floating... no obstruction, no bonds, no thoughts, no emotions. He is absolutely and completely in a pure state of rest. The thought then comes to his mind, *I will myself to remove this cloak.*

Remaining in this state for a moment, he hears Paul's voice. "Very good. Now, open your eyes and take the action."

A bit bewildered and disoriented to be back in visual contact with Paul, he flounders momentarily with the part about taking the action. Looking down at the cloak again, he states, "Sorry, Paul. I have to ask again. Where do I start?"

Paul answers, "Grasp the cloak with your hands and take the action of removing it."

Following Paul's guidance, Peter reaches forward and grasps a portion of the cloak in each hand and pulls, and to his amazement, the cloak parts very easily. With a single motion, almost as though he had performed this action before, he sweeps the cloak off himself completely. Instantly, there are all sorts of subtle sounds, lights, and energies. Peter stands rigid as he allows himself to experience all of these reactions to the removal of Zachary's cloak.

Paul, all the while studying Peter an arm's length away, asks, "Are you well? What are you are experiencing?"

"There is this remarkable difference somehow. I now feel much more... well, *here*. I don't know how else to explain it to you, Paul. It's as though I feel... like this bench here... more real. When I had Zachary's cloak on, I felt unbridled, like I wasn't subject to any forces. I was completely free. It isn't that I feel unpleasant now in any way. I just feel different. Without the cloak, I feel all of the colors here in the Garden. I can feel all of the energies, and I can hear and see and sense many things that I didn't quite notice when I had Zachary's cloak on."

Paul reaches out a hand indicating that Peter seat himself again. As Peter does, he carefully, and even fondly, straightens Zachary's cloak and folds it over his right forearm. Having straightened the cloak, much in the manner as he himself had observed Zachary doing, he turns again to Paul, who is smiling understandingly at him and waiting patiently. "Is the cloak necessary, Paul?"

"You see, Peter, that cloak has a way of preserving your integrity. To a degree, it acts as a filter. It acts as a reflector, something which interacts with the forces prevalent in the realm in which you are expressed. It is a shelter of sorts. That type of sheltering effect has a multiplicity of purposes, the primary of which is to preserve the realm and to simultaneously preserve you.

"Not that you would *need* to be preserved from any sort of harm, or that the realm in which you were present could be altered in any way. It is rather that it would preserve the vibrations, the thought-forms, the energies, and the intents and purposes of both you and the realm in which you would be expressed at that time.

"When you removed the cloak, you resumed your own expression, or spiritual cloak, which is much more attuned to this realm. All energies, all expressions in this realm, this garden place, are attuned to you. Therefore, you have a communication link or mechanism link between you and this realm. Is that making sense to you?"

Peter listens intently as Paul explains some of the characteristics of the cloak. Nodding an affirmation, "Yes, I believe I grasp the concept. Of course, I have quite a few questions about the specifics, but could you just go on for a time? I am really enjoying listening to you. It's as though you are speaking not only *to* me but, somehow or other *within* me. You know… like you did in Wilbur's realm there for a time?"

"I understand. I will continue, but feel free to interrupt or question at any point. The cloak is comprised of spiritual achievements on the part of Zachary, and as you might have surmised, they are many and note-worthy. Thus, the spirituality of Zachary is typified in the expression of his cloak. It is the outer expression of Zachary in any realm of finite expression where such expression can be perceived and interacted with. Literally speaking, Zachary is the source of that cloak's power. The beautiful cloak or robe-like garment as you have there over your arm is Zachary. Making sense?"

Peter simply nods. Silence passes for several moments as he continues to ponder and Paul anticipates a forthcoming question. "I'm beginning to get the distinct impression here, Paul, that this Zachary is somebody very special. I don't mean to slight anyone else, but it sure does appear from what you've said, and from the way he seems to be able to… well, manage things, that he has certain… what could I call them… uh… privileges?"

With a wide smile, Paul, responds, "Indeed, that is so,

but they aren't privileges that were idly given to him, nor that are given to him and denied to others. They are privileges of his achievements of spiritual awareness. Zachary has literally earned every, I might call it, ounce of energy that you feel and know to be in that cloak. There's not a thing that is a part of his spiritual cloak that Zachary hasn't carefully and thoroughly experienced and brought home to his spiritual being."

"How did he do that exactly, Paul?"

"In a variety of ways. Not the least of which were many sojourns involving the Earth, just as you have recently experienced."

"Really? You mean Zachary was on Earth, too? I wouldn't have thought that. He seems somehow above that. Yet, now that I think about it, I can't imagine he developed his wit and his ability to share insights without some interaction with others like myself. How did he gain that, anyway?"

Smiling even more broadly, Paul answers, "I guess it could be said that he gained that through trial and error. He actually worked very diligently... not unlike, for example, Wilbur. He focused much of his attention on developing an understanding of the nature of God, and how to express that nature to others. Particularly noteworthy have been his efforts on Earth and in other realms. So, perhaps you have a better understanding now of what I mean when I say that he did not simply come by them idly, but through serious dedication and effort. The Zachary you know today is far different than the Zachary who walked on Earth many, many Earth years past... hundreds, thousands, and more."

"Wow! That is fascinating."

Paul allows Peter space to ponder this.

After awhile, Peter asks, "Tell me, Paul. Does this cloak still, even though he's not here, somehow or other... you said it provides the equivalency of Zachary's spiritual achievement. You mean just by having this cloak over my arm, I have that potential right here over my arm?"

"In a manner of speaking, yes. But there's a small matter that needs to be identified here, and that is quite simply, one needs to know how to use it."

"I knew it. There's always a catch. We always had them on Earth, but I would have thought better of it here," jokes Peter, and with that, he bursts aloud into laughter, creating a melodious sound, shared and echoed by Paul of course.

They spent some time thereafter in conversation, discussing these and similar matters.

At this point, then, slightly further along, Peter asks, "Paul, let me turn for a moment to something else that's been on my mind. I know I just came from the Earth not very long ago. By the way, how do you measure time here, anyway?"

Paul answers, "Actually, any way you would prefer, but it's not an important issue here."

Thinking on that for a moment, Peter casts off other questions he has about that and continues on. "Well, back to my growing question here... Since I left there, I can recall some things about Earth, yet many things are no longer in my memory. Occasionally, when you or Zachary bring up a point, I can remember a similar situation from my time there, but all in all I don't remember much about my life there."

Paul, more serious now, straightens up and sits erect. "Peter, do you recall passing through the various colors?"

Peter reflects only for a moment and then responds comparatively quickly, "Yes, I remember those."

"The process you went through – passing through those colors and ultimately arriving at a point of what we call spiritual sleep – is a mechanism which functions very much like a veil. It is a veil of separateness, which preserves and nurtures the consciousness of each soul. By passing through the colors you saw, you were actually passing through the last remaining vestiges of your strongest emotional bonds to Earth. Having completed that, you entered into your spiritual sleep and emerged, balanced, in this realm.

"Perhaps the greatest parallel I could draw which would be familiar to you is the process you know of as birth. As souls are born into the realm of Earth, they pass through this veil – perhaps called a veil of darkness because it is comprised of all colors, all sound, all vibrations – and they are then allowed the opportunity to go forward to seek out their individual works and purposes for that sojourn or incarnation in the Earth.

"Upon completion of their time on Earth, they pass back through that veil... in essence, unburdening, un-limiting themselves to take up an incarnative experience here, though the word 'incarnate' implies a physical body. Here, an incarnative experience is an expression of consciousness, which is not limited in any way as a physical form would be.

"At some point in the future, as we progress further, you will be capable of reaching back into your soul consciousness, and be able to recall any and all of those experiences and associations which are a part of your just concluded incarnation on Earth. As a matter of fact, you could do so right at this moment, if you wish to. Do you?"

Peter, detecting a sense of significance in Paul's comment, pauses and turns inward, again visible by dancing lights and crackling sound upon his cloak. Paul waits a moment, and Peter emerges from his movement inward, and responds, "No, Paul, I don't believe I want to do that at this point. I find it very curious, and even a bit luring, but it's as though I have another me inside, telling me that perhaps now is not the best time to explore any of that."

Smiling at Peter's growing awareness, but deliberately being somewhat serious out of respect for Peter, Paul responds, "In fact, Peter, you have just that... an inner consciousness. That is still perhaps a bit beyond your comprehension at this point, but it is of no great concern for you now, for in times ahead, that too will come into full understanding for you."

Jingle-jingle… the sound subtle at first, then growing, intensifying… jingle, jingle, jingle.

Immediately Peter straightens himself and turns, half-jumping from the bench, to look off in the distance from whence he detects the sound.

The sound continues to grow and there, sure enough, comes Zachary, bobbing up and down, as though he were bouncing up the hillside, to where Paul and Peter are. "Hello there, everyone," he calls. "How are things going?"

Paul comments mirthfully, "They'll be better when you turn that jingling off."

Zachary, with a notable air of deliberate gesturing, swirls his hand upward above himself, and the sound stops instantly. "Sorry about that. I keep forgetting to turn it off. Thought I was doing well just remembering to turn it on." With that, he chuckles a bit, inspiring Peter to do the same.

"Gosh, I'm glad to see you, Zachary."

"Same here, Pete."

"Yes, indeed, Zachary. We were just speaking of you and your cloak… your gift to Peter."

"Well, how's it fitting?" Zachary inquires of Peter. "I notice you have it off. Was it troubling you? I can make an adjustment here or there, you know. Fitting too tight or something?"

Slightly embarrassed at Zachary's concern, Peter looks back at Paul somewhat helplessly.

Paul comes to the rescue, "No, we were just discussing the nature of the cloak, and I suggested to Peter that he might want to remove it to experience the difference."

"Excellent idea!" exclaims Zachary. "No better way to learn about one's potential than to explore the dimensions of it. I think it's good to look at our limitations. Why, I always say, 'Once one knows where one is, it's much easier to determine where one is going'. But if you don't know where you are, how in the world can you figure out where to go?

Wouldn't you agree, Pete?" Zachary breaks into a big smile and gives Peter an exaggerated wink, which relaxes him.

Peter nods. "Paul's been telling me you're quite accomplished in many areas, Zack."

"Well, don't let Paul convince you of too much. After all, I'm no better or lesser than anyone else here. Perhaps a bit more willing to experiment, mind you... but I haven't anything *magical*. Right, Paul?"

"If you say so, Zachary, then certainly that is correct."

"Well, Pete, would you like to explore a little more and perhaps even do a bit of experimenting on your own?"

"Just what do you mean by that, Zack?" queries Peter. "I don't have the confidence to do much experimenting here. Matter of fact, I have more questions than I have confidence."

With that, they all chuckle, and Zachary picks up the conversation again with the comment. "Well, first of all, how about putting my cloak back on?"

"Uh, sure, Zack. I only took it off to experience the difference."

"Good enough," with which Zachary steps forward, removes the cloak from over Peter's arm, and in a swift circular swishing motion, wraps Peter with it again.

Peter is standing there, a bit in awe of the swiftness and preciseness of Zachary's activities. "Zack, could I ask you a question?"

"Sure, Pete. Ask whatever you'd like."

"Just how do you put this on so quickly, and how does it fasten?"

Zachary, feigning a lack of comprehension, responds, "Fasten? What do you mean, fasten?"

Peter, stumbling just a bit, states, "Well, uh... you know... buttons. Or, uh... zippers. How's it... stay on me?"

"Oh, that. Well, it's not fastened to you, Pete. It's placed over you. You can remove it in the twinkling of an eye, as you say there on Earth. It's quite a simple matter.

Although… hmm… that might be a good idea. Buttons. Zippers. We'll have to think about that," with which he chuckles softly, followed by Paul."

Still appearing somewhat perplexed, pondering, Peter continues, "But, you made a simple swirling motion, and as I look down at myself, the cloak is perfectly in place."

Zachary interrupts with, "Hmm… Here, let me see something. Looks to me as though it needs some adjustment." Stepping forward, he goes through the brushing, whisking, straightening motions, which Peter has come to understand and expect. "Okay, how's that now, Pete? Better?"

"Why, yes. I thought the cloak was feeling great before, but after you did whatever it was you did, it feels even better. What did you do, anyway?"

With a note of seriousness Peter has not seen from Zachary very often, Zachary looks Peter in the eyes. "I am simply harmonizing myself with you. My cloak and yours, in effect, have become as one." Realizing his tone has become serious, Zachary quickly adds, "But that's, you know… like layers on an onion. Peel one off and there's always another."

Paul bursts into laughter as does Peter, and they enjoy the sound and elevation of the power released by that expression of joy.

"Well," comments Zachary after a bit, "I have a little business to take care of. You know, another brief journey. Care to go along again?"

Peter, his curiosity now piqued, asks, "Are we going to see Wilbur again?"

"Precisely. My, how astute you've become. Goodness, Paul, you are doing a good job with Pete. He's becoming more and more aware each time I see him."

"I'm only doing what comes naturally. Just being a friend and sharing."

"Well, nonetheless, you've done a good job. Will you be joining us, Paul?"

"Certainly."

With that, Zachary and Paul move swiftly to either side of Peter and off they go, each with an arm over Peter's shoulder. Zachary falls into what could best be described as a sort of bouncing, rolling canter, and Peter attempts to emulate it, as does Paul.

Zachary looks to Peter and then at Paul. "How about a bit of traveling music?" Before either of them can respond, Zachary extends his left hand up into the air, spins it, and immediately comes the jingling sound which has become the hallmark of Zachary's impending approach or departure.

Obviously pleased and delighted to be a part of this, Peter bounces all the more, as does Paul, as they pass into what appears to be a brilliant white, cloud-like formation.

All the while, the jingling and the good-natured cheer can be heard coming from our trio, and in what seems to be the passage of only several moments they emerge, once again, into the Crystal Worker's Realm.

Peter's stride falls out of cadence with the other two as he looks about Wilbur's realm, having decided this time he will be much more observant and ask many more questions. "Zachary, how did we get here? Exactly what took place?"

"Nothing to it, Pete. It's just the movement from one realm of expression, one level of consciousness, to another. What we passed through, that you saw as a sort of fluffy white cloud, is merely what we'd call a neutral zone, or a neutral pathway between the realms. It's like a separation point, a veil of sorts, if you see…"

Peter interrupts, pleased that he has some knowledge with which to respond to Zachary. "Oh, I know what you mean. Paul and I were talking about that. It's like the veils that separate different realms of consciousness, like he called the veil of… What was it now? Colors, or… darkness between the Earth and our garden place.

"That's it precisely," answers Zachary. "Just birds of a

feather... same type of thing. Good observation, Pete." Continuing to nudge Peter forward, Zachary's movement quickens and they cover the ground between them and the structure off in the distance with remarkable speed and ease.

As they do so, once again Peter takes note of the landscape. "Zachary? Paul? The flowers and colors are not as brilliant as they are in our Garden Realm. Why is that?"

"Poor gardening staff, I guess," Zachary offers offhandedly.

Paul chuckles, "He's teasing, again, Peter. Actually, it has to do with the narrow focus of the consciousness of those in this realm. Since they aren't focusing their consciousness more broadly, things such as this don't get the same amount of... well, we could call it attention or balance, as they do in our realm."

Reflecting on that thought for a moment, Peter counters with, "Well, why don't they focus more broadly, as you said? If they don't know about it, or don't know how to do it, why don't you and Zachary help them?"

There is silence for a moment, after which Zachary replies, "Well, perhaps we shall, Pete, perhaps we shall... but all in good time. A person needs to be mindful of whom they work for, and uh... follow the rules, so to say. These people haven't asked, and it would be impolite to force upon them anything that they're not ready for or seeking. Do you understand what I am saying?"

"Well, I guess I do, for the most part," but before Peter realizes it, they have reached the entrance to the great structure once again. Quickly studying its construction, Peter remarks, "My! This is wonderful work. Just like the benches in our garden. Who did this work?"

Zachary answers, "They did."

"They who?"

"They... the ones we're going to see inside here, in the hall. Let's go in. Is that okay with you, Peter?"

"Well, uh… sure, I guess so."

They enter the hall, and Peter once again surveys the very large chamber… its ornateness, the various tables and resting places, the writing apparati, and his gaze comes to rest upon a number of the entities. As before, he is first drawn to the appearance of their cloaks.

In a subdued voice, so as not to disturb them, Peter leans towards Zachary, and asks in a half-whisper, "I know I asked some questions about this before, but why is it their cloaks look the way they do?"

Zachary, emulating Peter, leans his head to the side and whispers, "Their choice."

Puzzled, Peter asks both Zachary and Paul this time, "Yes, but why are their cloaks so different from ours?" Looking down as he speaks, he sees the shimmering, blue-white effervescence of Zachary's cloak upon himself. Glancing from one side to the other, he sees the same, almost identical effervescence from both of his colleagues.

"Why don't I take a moment to answer your question, Peter. I know Zachary has a bit of work to do."

"That's right. Have to be about my… chores, borrowing a term from the Earth," he chuckles. "I'll be back soon." With that, Zachary moves to the other side of the hall.

Peter, again studying Zachary as he departs, feels the familiar feeling as in the previous journey here, as though a part of himself is leaving. "What is that feeling I have as Zachary leaves?" Peter asks quietly.

"It is the bond between you and Zachary, largely because you have on his cloak. So, you are connected, in a manner of speaking, and now it is as though a part of you is some distance away. This can create a temporary feeling of incompleteness or loss, which you are recalling from your previous Earth experience. That has to do with the one emotion that we had a bit of difficulty with – represented by the red color – when we passed through it. Do you recall?"

Instantly, some mixed reactions occur within Peter, and he answers in a clipped voice, "Oh, yes, I do. I seemed to have a reaction inside me."

"The feeling which comes over you when you see Zachary leave is similar to the feeling which occurred in you when we were passing through the red color. But perhaps now is not the best time to go further into this. We can certainly come back to this discussion later, if you have more questions. Is this acceptable to you, Peter?"

"Yes, thank you."

"For now, let's turn to your question about the cloak. Here's our friend, still working at the table. Remember him?"

"Yes. I really like him. Don't you? He looks like a very nice person. I'm sorry he can't see us. I'd certainly like to meet him and just... you know, have a chat with him."

"Would you, really?"

"Really what?"

"What you said. Would you really like to meet him and extend some neighborly... whatever you called it?"

"Well, uh... yes. I would, Paul. As I said, he looks like a nice fellow."

"Well, then, so be it. Speak to him."

"What?"

"Just as I said. Speak to him."

"Well... I thought he couldn't hear us, or see us."

"Try it. Speak to him. His name is David."

Obviously unsettled, concerned now about what exactly he might say, Peter leans forward, being careful not to disrupt his work. "Good day to you, sir. How are you?"

Peter has all he can do to keep his countenance balanced and not draw within himself. He realizes then that he is calmed and feels a sense of constant balance, and as he does, he sees that Paul has his hand on his right shoulder.

Smiling, Paul continues to encourage, "Well, go ahead. Talk with him, as you said."

Flustered and excited at the same time, Peter stammers, "Well, David, uh... my name is Pete... or Peter. I'm, uh... I'm visiting here, and uh... I couldn't help but admire your work."

Obviously pleased, David stands and motions to Peter, "Here, Peter. Come around here and seat yourself by me, and I'll show you what I'm doing."

Swiftly looking back at Paul, Peter gets a nod and a smile of approval, and so he awkwardly moves around the table and seats himself beside David.

Leaning forward, David resumes his work. "I'm not sure how much you know about this work, Peter, so forgive me if I assume anything. I'll just start where I am here, and tell you briefly what I'm doing."

"Well, that sounds very nice," answers Peter, courteously. "I'll just listen."

Grinning, Paul stands across from Peter, knowing full well that Peter has no idea what is about to transpire.

With that, David reaches towards a lovely, velvet-like fabric on which he has several lights focused upon what appears to be a crystal. Peter notices that the lights aren't connected to anything. They have a rectangular-like outer covering, tapering off to something that looks pointed, pyramidal almost, at the other end. "You see, we are more or less irradiating this crystal as a means of communication with the Earth. God has granted us many blessings here, including being allowed to answer prayers from Earth. We are working with people there who provide help to those who have lost their way, or are dis-eased, or have become entrapped in the illusion of their own nature.

"So we use these devices to irradiate the crystals. They are a common vibration to those in the Earth realm, and therefore, through them we are capable of transmitting, in a manner of speaking, energy, prayer, and power back to them. I have nearly completed work on this crystal, at which point I will give it to one or two of the others, and they will work with it in conjunction with several people on Earth, who are called healers or practitioners. Then, the crystal here can provide the healers an energy flow, as they have the need, that will enable the balancing of errant energies in their patients." At this point, David pauses.

Peter is speechless, in total awe and wonder. Looking up to Paul and then back down at the crystal, he can only find a very small voice with which to speak, and the words come out, "That is absolutely incredible."

David nods and smiles. "Yes, it is, isn't it? One can't help but wonder at the magnitude and power of God. We are so grateful and so blessed here, Peter, that I find sometimes that we have become totally engrossed in this work, often to the exclusion of other opportunities and blessings. We take turns in building the thought-form of our environment and the terrain around it, but I must be among the first to admit that we don't give them nearly enough of our attention. The more we work with these crystals, and the building of these thought-forms and the transmission of response in God's name to requests for prayers, the more we are drawn into that and away from other activities."

Totally inundated by a sense of admiration, compassion, and wonder, Peter again responds in a very small voice, "That is quite admirable and marvelous. How fortunate you are. And how fortunate the Earth is, to have you."

Hearing a bit of jingling, Peter looks up to see Zachary standing beside him. "Hello, David. How are things today?"

"Quite well, Zachary. How nice to see you again. Is Peter a friend of yours?"

"Oh, yes, indeed," answers Zachary, smiling at Peter. "We are old friends. Pete's going to be helping Wilbur. Perhaps you can help them both somewhat, if you have time."

David smiles very broadly, "Oh, most assuredly,

Zachary. You know, anything that I can do to help you or your friends, you have only to ask. I would consider it an honor, a privilege, and a joy," and he reaches out to touch Peter on the shoulder.

Peter quickly looks at Paul, remembering how Paul had interceded when Wilbur had reached out to touch him before. He tenses, waiting for something similar to occur, but Paul and Zachary make no such move and simply continue to stand, smiling gently at Peter.

David's hand makes contact with Peter just below his neck, mid-shoulder, and Peter feels an instantaneous burst of illumination and light, a sense of love, compassion, and joy, unlike anything he has recalled to this point. He turns to look into David's eyes.

David very calmly answers his look with, "I have truly enjoyed your visit, Peter, and I hope you will return often and call upon me if I can be of any assistance at any time. And I thank you for your kindness to my friend Wilbur, in whatever way you are intending to assist him. He is a wonderful person and we all love him very much, so we thank you for coming to be a companion or aide to him."

David, then, removes his hand from Peter's shoulder, and stands and bows ever so slightly towards Paul and Zachary, and then in turn to Peter.

Zachary reaches over and, taking Peter by the arm, essentially lifts him from his chair. Peter, who is still reeling in wonder from this experience, more or less floats along at Zachary's side.

As they move back to the center of the room, Zachary looks over at Peter. "Interesting chap, wouldn't you say?"

Barely containing his strong desire to turn inward, but concerned that doing so might disrupt this realm, Peter answers weakly, "That's the understatement of the day, Zack."

Paul chuckles and then states, "Wilbur's over there, waving at us. Why don't we go over and say hello to him."

"Good idea," and Zachary strides up to Wilbur, extending his arms in the open invitation of an embrace.

Peter, somewhat apprehensive, lags behind and approaches slowly. He marvels at what he perceives, for as Zachary and Wilbur embrace and gently pat one another on the back, lights are dancing forward and upward from Zachary's cloak and reaching around to envelope Wilbur and radiate off him. After they part, Peter can see that Wilbur is still retaining some of the light, the color, the energy, from Zachary's cloak.

Looking at Peter now, Wilbur extends his hand across his small worktable.

Peter quickly looks at Paul, questioningly. Receiving a nod, Peter slowly moves forward and extends his hand. As their hands make contact, Peter notes that from his own cloak, similar lights dance forward and bounce upward and swiftly encompass Wilbur, just the same as they did when Zachary embraced him.

Smiling and nodding, with his little bow, Wilbur states, "How nice to see you again, Peter. Thank you for coming to visit, and thank you for answering my prayer."

As their hands part, Peter is bewildered, for he knows not in any sense how he might have answered Wilbur's prayer. He wouldn't even know what the mechanism would be, nor has he ever heard a prayer coming from anywhere all the time he has been in the Garden Realm.

Zachary, standing behind Wilbur, raises a finger to his mouth, indicating to Peter not to speak. Then, removing his finger, he places his hands behind his back, and rocks back and forth, smiling broadly at Peter.

As though none of this is transpiring, Wilbur carries on conversing with Peter. "I took your idea of making these changes here, and I think it will work wonderfully. We've had someone on Earth get much better as the result."

Looking at what Wilbur is pointing to, Peter can see

another very beautiful crystal. Many colors dance from within it, particularly dominant is a brilliant golden yellow.

Instantly, Peter recalls the color as the same one which popped forth from his fingertip during his experiments with Zachary, which later became the butterfly. Suddenly realizing that something has transpired here that involves him, he looks up at Zachary who is still watching him, smiling, nodding, and indicating with a shrug of his shoulders that simple acceptance is the rule.

Turning back to Wilbur, Peter, a little embarrassed, answers with a soft uncertainty, "Uh… It was, uh… nothing at all, Wilbur. I'm sure that whatever you have before you, and whatever your accomplishments are your own making."

Wilbur, illuminated now by the encouragement from Peter, states, "Just what I would have expected you to say. You are every bit the spiritual entity that Zachary has told me you were. Again, I thank you. I am so pleased you came to visit. But if you'll excuse me, I'll go back to work here. There is more need that has come to me to answer, and I don't want to miss the opportunity. I'm sure you understand."

Zachary steps forward now. "Indeed, we do, Wilbur. We wouldn't keep you from your work under any circumstances. Let us know if we can help you any further. We hope to come and see you again very soon," and Zachary bows to honor Wilbur's bow, and they exchange bows among them.

Swiftly then, Zachary and Paul once again each grasp one of Peter's arms, and off they go. As they pass by David's place of work, all nod and wave to him and he reciprocates with a large smile.

Departing the great structure and looking about, Peter remembers what David had stated about the ill-kept grounds and their focus upon their work.

As they reach the area of the cloud-like mist, once again Zachary steps forward in front of Peter, and Paul falls in behind with a hand extended to rest upon Peter's shoulder, and they enter the mist, notably less brilliant than it was when they came into this realm.

Soon, they emerge once again in the Garden Realm, bathed by the brilliant colors and light, and the harmonized sounds and splendor of the existence there.

Zachary immediately walks over to a lush expanse of the colorfully dotted flower-filled knoll and reclines upon it, once again propping himself up on one elbow. "Good journey. Good work. I'm very proud of you, Pete. Aren't you, Paul?"

Paul smiles and nods, "Yes, indeed. You have done very well, Peter, especially considering, as both Zachary and I know, that you weren't really aware of what was transpiring. Now I might suggest that you take some time to balance, and when you are ready, we'll discuss this to whatever depth you'd wish."

As you move deeper into the experience of this work, remember… there is a Peter, a Zachary, a Paul, a David, a Wilbur, within each of you.

CHAPTER 7

The Universe Within
SEPTEMBER 9, 1990

In that which follows next, we should think you will note the occurrence of several events which will answer some of your questions, and perhaps open for you areas of awareness as yet not explored in the current incarnation. The significance of our definition here of the terrain or landscape will come to bear in time. Let it form an image, a thought-pattern in your mind, spiritually speaking, as we turn now to Paul, who nods to us that Peter is returning to a conscious state in this realm, The Garden.

Paul is leaned back upon the lush green expanse of a rolling summit dotted with brilliant arrays of flowers and other plant life, all seemingly reaching forth with exuberance to offer their fragrance, their color, and to interact with one another in a harmonious collage of those essences.

Above this are beautiful pastel blues, indicative of the loving compassion and ever-present force of the power of God's grace. Round and about them, the terrain flows with a sense of continuity and blending, harmonically intertwining, varying shades and hues of greens and other colors, seemingly carefully placed as though an architect of master distinction had literally created and organized the entire realm as you have come to know it.

Off in the distance from where Paul and Peter are inclined, looking downwards along the path from which Zachary has approached, is a structure to the right. The structure has a pearly iridescence to it, glowing in a shimmering radiance or silver-white luminosity. This structure has always been present. In this current experience, this meeting, Peter will discover it—or, as it were, in the inimitable style of friend Zachary, he will be introduced to it.

One hundred eighty degrees in the opposite direction, the pathway slopes gently downward and moves off into the distance into what appears to be the very massive white cloud-like substance that Peter, Paul, and Zachary embarked through or upon to reach Wilbur's realm.

Here, about Paul and Peter, in a very neat, semi-circular pattern, are the benches Peter considered to be so wonderfully crafted, and upon one of which Zachary inclined himself in his pixie-like manner.

Peter, rubbing his eyes a bit, perhaps out of habit left over from Earth, blinks and greets Paul. "Hello again, Paul."

Paul smiles warmly at him, "You appeared to be resting very well, Peter. Are you in a good state? Are you well at this time?"

Now seated somewhat erectly, Peter places a hand upon his forehead and brow, rubbing these just a bit as well. "An odd thing seems to be lingering in my mind, Paul. If it's okay, I'd like to get your perspective on it. I don't recall it occurring in any of my earlier... what did you call them... spiritual balancing times?"

Paul, with a more serious expression on his face and in his countenance, comes to a cross-legged position in front of Peter, and smiles reassuringly. "Just as you please, Peter. Always remember that we are more than happy, all of us here, to help you in any way that we can and to answer any questions that you might have. What is troubling you? Is there something you are concerned about?"

Peter is looking down at the greenery upon which he rests, running his hand back and forth over the grass, noting as he does the slight tingling and exhilarating feeling that comes from it, just as in the past. It is as though the very environment, even every blade of grass, is reassuring and supporting him, contributing to his well-being.

"Well, Paul, it's… as best I can describe it, like a dream. I recall that sometimes in the Earth realm, I'd wake up in the morning and have all of these very vivid memories of things I had done and places I had gone. I never put too much stock in them, except on several occasions when some of them later came true. I know there is a term for that sort of thing, but they were particularly significant for me… as I guess you know, since you seem to know a great deal about me and my past lifetime. Do you?"

Paul simply nods, warmly.

"Well, this time I seemed to recall – very vividly mind you – an experience, a dream I guess. I had gone back to Earth. In the dream, I saw myself walking around just as though I was in a… well, a real physical body once again. I walked up and down some of the streets like those I had walked on when I was… well… you know. This is all very confusing to relate. Everything seems to be so strange."

Peter pauses a moment, fidgeting with several of the brightly colored flowers in the grass near his hand. "I thought it was very curious. Somehow or other I knew what I was doing the whole time. I decided I'd go look up some old friends and… you know, visit the old office and that sort of thing. No different than a lot of dreams I had on Earth. All I had to do was think about being in my old office and, bang! I was there, standing right there in the waiting room, and all the things that I remembered were pretty much still there, though some of them had been moved. But I didn't see anyone. Anyway, I went in.

"There was my old desk, and my chair, and the aquarium over there on the bookcase. I even noticed that the fish still looked healthy. Things were all pretty much as I remember them, or I guess I could say, as they were when I left. But one thing really had an impact on me, Paul… really hit me hard."

Paul, showing interest and concern, answers, "Would you care to talk about it some more, Peter? Do you think that would help?"

"Well, I guess so. I don't know what to make of it. I guess dreams are like that here or in the Earth. I mean, a dream is a dream, I guess. But in this one, I looked on my desk and there was the big 8x10 photograph of my family. It was really strange, Paul. While I was looking at the photo, for a moment it was as though someone had poured a great bucket of some sort of warm, sticky fluid all over me, like hot, transparent paste or something like that. I felt like, if I reached out and held the photograph, I wouldn't be able to let go of it, like maybe it would have stuck to me. Then I remembered, even in the middle of this dream, what you had told me in our earlier conversations. So, I just observed. It was really difficult, though. I wanted to reach out and touch the photograph and, more or less, touch my family as well."

Looking down, Paul asks, "Is there anything else you can recall, Peter?"

Peter is still fidgeting with the flowers under his fingertips. "Well, I don't know. Maybe you know about this, too. I'm not sure how you know the things you do, Paul. Not that I mind your knowing. In fact, I'm, glad you do. Saves a lot of time, not needing to tell you everything about myself. Anyway, maybe you know about this, too… Just about that point in the dream, I felt someone touch my elbow… my right elbow. I turned, and there you were. You smiled at me, and suddenly I felt okay. The sticky, warm sensation left immediately, and suddenly everything was gone and I was in that sort of white cloudy mist… you know, that Zachary and you and I traveled in to see Wilbur.

"But this time, Paul, it was very different. It was sort of translucent but still bright white, and I could see through to the end of it to this incredibly beautiful, brilliant light. You didn't say anything to me, but somehow I knew what you were thinking, and I just followed that sort of internal knowing. Still holding my elbow, you lifted me up somehow, and we moved with awesome speed through some kind of... well, I guess it was like a chamber or a tube or something of that sort... smack into that bright white light. Just smack into it. It was such an exhilarating feeling... like a Fourth of July fireworks, except that instead of loud banging, the fireworks went off with a symphony of tones and colors that sent little rivers of light and sound all through me.

"I was so happy, exuberant, and I just sort of rolled around in this color and light as it cascaded all over us. Oh, Paul, it's one of the grandest feelings I think I can ever remember. We were laughing and giggling and throwing little balls of light and color up into the air, and each time we did, they'd make sounds that were just beautiful. That went on for I don't know how long. But now, as I look back on it, it seemed to take everything away... all of the concerns and doubts and feelings that I was beginning to have while standing in my old office looking at the photograph." With that last comment, Peter looks down and fidgets with the grass and flowers all the more.

Paul looks up at Peter, and reaches out and touches him on the shoulder.

As Peter looks up to meet Paul's gaze, he can see the warmth and gentle compassion that radiates from Paul's face, and he can actually see the fireworks – the collage of sound and color and light – all over again, as though Paul's eyes are projecting it back into his mind, beaming the memory back inside his head.

Peter remains in his state of wonder, reveling in the recollection of that jubilant experience once again, stopping only when Paul removes his hand from his shoulder.

Blinking several times, Peter, still looking at Paul,

whose gaze is unwavering and as gentle and warm as ever, states, "Incredible! How did you do that? What just took place? What's happening, anyway?"

Paul pauses a moment as though anticipating something, leans slightly, and glances back down the hill over Peter's left shoulder. In that instant, comes the familiar jingle-jangling sound.

Exuberantly, Peter half rolls, half turns, and stands in one swift motion, to look for his friend, Zachary. This time, as he perceives Zachary coming from off in the distance, he notes that Zachary is bouncing along the pathway with a new zest, almost as though he were a ballet performer not bound to the Earth by the force of gravity... his leaps, his movements, swift, graceful and flowing.

In just a few moments, Zachary's leaping stride brings him before Peter and Paul. "Hello, there, good friends, how are you doing today? Well, I hope. My, have I been busy. Lots to tell you about, and lots of things to do... if you'd be interested, Pete," casting a knowing wink to Peter.

A bit disarmed in view of the conversation he has just had with Paul, Peter turns swiftly to look at Paul.

Paul, nodding a signal of reassurance, turns to look at Zachary, and states, "Well, Zachary, we were just about to discuss Peter's dream."

"You don't say. Had a dream, did you, Pete? I just love to hear dreams. You know, I could spend days listening to people's dreams. They always tell one so much about the person." Zachary places himself at Peter's side, and places an arm on his shoulder. He makes a motion of collapsing to the ground, dragging Peter down with him as he does, but with an unexpected gracefulness. Nonetheless, Peter is amused at this, which obviously pleases Zachary.

Taking his arm down from Peter, Zachary crosses his legs as though imitating Paul and places his hands in his lap. "Well then, let's hear about the dream. Where were you?

What were you doing? Who were you? Were there others there? Were you there long? What took place? Come on. Don't keep me in suspense. Let's hear about it."

Inspired by Zachary's enthusiasm and simultaneously amused by his approach, Peter relaxes and freely relates the entire sum and substance of what he recalls of the dream, just as he had told it to Paul. Turning to Zachary, "And you know what Paul did after I told him that?"

Acting concerned, Zachary responds, "No. What did he do?" and looks sternly at Paul, who responds by looking down to hide his humor at Zachary's antics.

"Well, he put a hand on my shoulder, and looked me right in the eye, and when he did, I saw that entire last part all over again, almost as though I was reliving it."

Now feigning surprise and acting as though he has no knowledge of this, Zachary swiftly moves himself to a position that forms a triangle pattern between he, Peter, and Paul. "That's incredible! How did you do that, Paul? Could you do it again? Pete, would you be willing to have him do that again? Maybe this time I could come along and see it, too," concluding a smile and a wink.

Peter, now much more astute, senses that Zachary is up to something again. Smiling at Zachary, he returns with, "I don't have a problem with it. In fact, I would relish going back there. I enjoyed it immensely. So, Zack, whatever it is you are up to this time, I'm game for it. Count me in."

"Bravo, my lad. You have real promise. I told them. I always told them, 'That Pete, he's the one to watch... a real sleeper. He's going places.' Didn't I tell them that, Paul?"

Struggling to contain himself from an outburst of laughter, Paul fidgets and, to hide his humor from Peter, looks down so far that only the top of his head is visible. "Yes, indeed you did, Zachary. Indeed you did."

"Well, how about it then, Paul? Let's take this trip. Show me what you showed Peter. He said it was okay."

Without further word, Paul places an arm on Peter's shoulder and another on Zachary's. Zachary, in turn, places his arms on Paul and Peter, and Peter follows suit.

Several moments pass. Neither Paul nor Zachary makes a move, and Peter looks nervously between them.

Finally, Zachary breaks the silence. "What happens next, Paul? Where'd you go from here?"

Smiling, Paul answers, "Well, I just looked into Peter's eyes."

With his impish grin, Zachary asks, "Well, then, whose eyes do I look into? Yours or his?"

Paul, amused at the absurdity of Zachary's question but without taking his eyes off Peter, answers, "Now, Zachary, it is Peter's dream, not mine. Look into his eyes."

Continuing to feign some lack of knowledge, Zachary answers, "Oh. Yes, of course. How silly of me. Uh... Pete, forgive me for staring, but that's the way Paul wants it. You heard him."

Having difficulty keeping any sense of sobriety, now, Peter begins to chuckle. They look from one to the other, and each begins to chuckle more and more until they are in uproarious laughter.

Instantly, they find themselves surrounded by the exact same environment, circumstances, and conditions as Peter related to Paul regarding the dream. Colors are everywhere. They begin rolling about, arms interlocked, laughing, giggling, standing, then sitting, then rolling about again, and spinning.

Finally, after a time, their laughter slows, and Peter, looking about, shouts out, "This is marvelous! Just marvelous! Can we stay here? Don't do anything now, Zack, to change this. You know, like the purple flowers, and don't let me make them go away... I'm not doubting. I do believe this. I know this is really happening."

With that, Zachary and Paul burst out with mirthful

laughter again, which Peter is once again caught up in, and they continue on with this uproarious, belly-whopper display. They roll about, up the colors and down the other side, their arms interlocked as though they had formed a miniature wheel, laughing and giggling like children. All the while, the colors seem to be imitating them, bouncing, dancing... lights, sound, fragrances, a collage of symphonic blending.

After a while, they come to a state of rest, bliss, looking from one to the other with an attitude of love that can only be described as the bond which exists between entities who share joyous laughter. Not at the expense of one to the other, not in the sense of having made fun of another or belittled or demeaned, but in the spontaneity of being a part of something so incredibly beautiful, that the beauty and pristine holy sanctity is uplifting so as to cause the spontaneity of laughter, a laughter of eternal joy. *If you in the Earth realm would like to sense, to feel, something similar to this, find a small child and just laugh with them, and you'll feel it, you'll feel the essence of what we are describing. Or gather together, and as a group say a prayer, meditate, and then just look at each other—and laugh.*

Still in this realm of beautiful light, still with their arms interlocked like Greek dancers or Cossacks, the light that is all-present seems to focus itself upon them, changing, becoming ordered and patterned. It seems to move around and across their arms and their shoulders, and slowly begins to increase and accelerate. As it does, different colors and hues come and go, and with them, different sounds, different essences, each one having the effect of illuminating the trio just a bit more. After a time, the color reaches a state of motion where it appears as though it is constant—yet we know it is in motion.

Paul looks at Peter and then at Zachary, and nods, and they know it is time to leave this realm. The instant that all three are aware and in agreement, they find themselves seated exactly where they began. But they are different now, for the light which was a part of their experience has somehow emblazoned itself into and upon them.

Paul slowly removes his arms from the others, and they look back and forth, each to the other, not speaking. Then Paul and Zachary place their hands, one upon the other, in their laps.

Peter, incredulously, looks at his hands and wiggles his fingers. Seeing rivulets of light radiating from each of them, he flexes his fingers and his hands in wonder, and looks up, first at Paul and then at Zachary, and smiles. Finally, after a while, he speaks. "How wonderful. How beautiful it is, my friends, to be here with you. I don't know what gift, what blessing you have just given me. I'm not so sure I even care why or how it came to be my privilege to have experienced it and to have whatever it is that is within me at this moment. All I can tell you is, from somewhere deep inside me I suddenly feel whole, complete. I feel so good, so wonderful."

Paul, obviously touched by Peter's comments, and Zachary too, visibly moved by the sincerity of Peter's expressions, both look at each other for several moments, and then they turn to look back at Peter. Paul is the first to speak, as Zachary looks down now and begins to brush his hand back and forth over the lushness beside him.

"Peter," Paul begins, "we're going to tell you some things now that we've waited to tell you—not because we were hiding them or concealing them from you, but because we felt from within our own inner guidance that it wasn't time. Zachary and I agree that you are prepared to have some greater perspective and concept of who and what you are, and what this new experience you are in is all about.

"We know you have often wondered about so many things, and we haven't given you the opportunity to ask the many questions that have occurred to you throughout our experiences here together. This was because we felt it important for you to experience more of them, so that you would then have a better grasp of our answers to your questions. So now we should like to share with you a bit more of this—who you are, what you are, where you are, and what lies ahead. How does that sound to you? Do you think you are ready to hear more?"

Peter, still taken by the raiment of color which continues to circulate around him, and obviously in very elated spirits, answers very softly, looking directly at Paul, "I am ready, Paul. I trust you and Zachary, and I know you know what's best for me. I don't know how I know that. I just know it. I don't think there have ever been two people that I have either trusted so unconditionally or loved as much and as unconditionally as I trust and love you both."

Moved by the sheer honesty and sincerity of Peter's comments, both Paul and Zachary look down for several long moments. Zachary continues to look down as Paul finally raises his eyes to make contact with Peter's, and states in just the same manner as Peter himself has spoken to them, "Peter, Zachary and I are honored by the comments you have just made to us and about us. We shall forever strive to be worthy recipients of such words of kindness and faith. In that same vein of truth and forthright honesty, may we now humbly offer to you these explanations and comments...

"It is not we, Peter, who have given you these great gifts. Rather, it is you who have given to us. It is not by our doing, that which you have just recently experienced; but rather by your doing, that we were enabled to share with you that joy, that wonder, and the love and compassion which came as the product of that shared experience."

Paul pauses, continuing to look into Peter's eyes. Peter is now sitting very still, listening intently and looking incredulously back at Paul, striving to grasp the meaning of what he is hearing. Paul casts a quick glance at Zachary, who is still looking down, brushing the grass, silent, quite out of character for the Zachary we know. "You see, Peter, Zachary and I are just workers here. We have seen your thoughts and we know what is in your heart, and we aren't really as you think us to be. We possess no great magical powers, and while it is true that we have come to a considerable degree of acceptance regarding the subject of our spirituality, we are no greater than you. To the contrary, in some respects we have much to learn from you."

Peter now looks quickly back and forth between Zachary and Paul. All the while, Zachary continues looking down, gently brushing the grass this way and that.

"Well, Paul, I don't know what to say. I don't exactly understand what you're telling me, and I'm quite certain you know that. As I said, I trust you. I believe in you. You are my friends. Could you explain more about what you mean?"

"Of course. We have every intention, not only of explaining to you, but of showing you."

"Showing me?" asks Peter. "You mean like what we just did?"

"Well, not quite exactly like that. This time it will be in a way that, perhaps, is more familiar to you, closer to what you remember at this point."

With that comment, Paul turns to Zachary and softly asks, "Zachary? Are you ready?"

Zachary pauses a moment and makes some kind of motions Peter can't quite grasp, as though he is putting the greenery back the way he found it before he began to caress it. He looks up at Paul and then glances quickly over to Peter.

Instantaneously, Peter sees in Zachary's eyes something he cannot recall ever having seen previously. It is as though in a microcosmic sense, what is radiating from Zachary's eyes is the same essence that he felt and experienced in their shared activity just previous, in the light.

Blinking several times, as though to break that connection between him and Peter in order to move on,

Zachary comments, "Sure. I'm ready. You know me. I'm always ready for an outing. How about you, Pete?"

This familiar return to the Zachary personality that Peter has come to be comfortable with, and to actually love and long for, rebalances Peter. All of the lights and colors they had previously experienced seem to find a place of rest on Peter, making him appear rather like an illuminated Christmas tree.

With that, Zachary rises to his feet, reaching out a hand to Peter and Paul, and with an effortless motion, swiftly pulls them to an upright position. Looking at Peter for a prolonged moment, Zachary gets that familiar twinkle in his eye, and with a wink, says, "Well, let's break some old myths. What do you say, Pete? Are you game?"

Peter returns Zachary's lighthearted mood. "Absolutely, Zack. I'm ready when you are. Shatter away."

Paul chuckles, and again the trio takes their familiar position of lining up in a row and wrapping arms around each other, and off they go.

As they do, Zachary turns to Peter and says, "This walking stuff is... what do you call it on Earth? Oh, yes... for the birds. ...Never did understand that expression, Pete. Sometime you'll have to explain some of those colloquialisms to me. Lots of them just don't make much sense. Is it that they're intended not to make sense, and that's what's humorous about them? Oh well, either way, like I said... this walking stuff is for the birds. Look over there. See that building?"

Peter looks in the direction Zachary is gesturing, and is somewhat startled because he hadn't noticed the building previously. "Why, yes! I see it. Gosh, I hadn't noticed that before."

Zachary grins eagerly, "Well, let's go over there. Okay with you?"

"Sure, Zack, I'd like to see it."

"Okay. The first myth we're going to shatter is: we don't walk places here. There's no need. Again, do you see the building?"

"Yes, I do. It's beautiful. You see it, Paul?"

"Why, yes," chuckles Paul. "I see it, too."

Somewhat embarrassed at his attempt to mimic Zachary's humor in his question to Paul, Peter quickly turns to Zachary to shift the attention, "What next?"

"Not much, Pete. But how about this... you see the building, you want to be there. Zing! We're there."

With that, Peter looks about in awe as he finds himself standing on the threshold of this wondrous structure, marveling at the great creation radiating luminosity from it at every turn, on every curve, on every corner. "This is awesome. Look how beautiful!"

"Yes, it is, if I do say so myself," Zachary answers.

"Wait a minute, Zack. Are you saying that you made this building?"

"Well, uh... yes and no, Pete. I made it, you made it, Paul made it, and all the others made it. If we made it, I made it. So, I guess you could say, yes, I made it." With that, Zachary has found humor in his own comments and begins a little dance, to the laughter of Paul and Peter.

Their humor is broken by the appearance of an entity at the top of the steps before them. Peter is startled, and turns swiftly to verify that both Paul and Zachary are still present. Reassured, he turns back to look upon the entity.

The figure seems normal, though perhaps a bit more luminous than he has seen in these realms. To explain that a bit better, the keeper of the Book of Wisdom and her companion were more luminous than Paul and Zachary and himself, and he had noted that mentally but hadn't queried about it. Now, as he notes that this entity has more luminosity, he equates this to the two females who had befriended him previously. Peter turns to see Zachary waving to the entity at the top of the stairs.

Speaking in a low voice, he asks, "Zachary, who is that? And, uh… they have the same radiance."

Zachary, still waving and looking up the stairs, speaks softly out of the side of his mouth, again imitating Peter, "Just who's 'they,' Pete? Who's the 'they' you're talking about?"

"Well uh, you know, the… the two… uh, ladies or girls… the one with the book and her friend, and now this fellow up there… they all have a sort of similar radiance."

Zachary, continuing to wave and look straight up the stairs, speaks again out of the side of his mouth, "I think you're on to something, Pete. Let's go up and see."

Without another word, Zachary scoops an arm into Peter's, while Paul does the same. In the twinkling of an eye, they find themselves standing before the entity.

The entity appears to be very warm, very gentle, and to have a wise and compassionate countenance. Peter marvels at the sense of timelessness that he emanates. There is nothing aged about his appearance. To the contrary, his appearance seems almost pristine, reminding him again of the two female entities, as though they were all devoid of such burdens as time and aging.

Because they are all just standing there, Peter glances awkwardly left and right from Zachary to Paul, and then back to the entity, who is all the while gently looking at Peter, not more than an arm and a half length directly in front of him. No longer able to bear the awkwardness of the moment, Peter stammers, "Hello. Uh… my name is Peter, and… uh, these are my friends. This is Zachary here and," motioning with his left hand, "this is Paul over here."

Dutifully, Zachary and then Paul nod and offer a small bow, which the entity acknowledges with a nod to each.

Extending his hand out to Peter, the entity then gestures towards the entrance of the structure, "We have been expecting you, Peter, and we warmly welcome you. Won't you enter?""

Very much out of balance at this point, and with a myriad of questions racing through his consciousness, Peter's cloak begins to crackle and sparkle. In embarrassment, he turns swiftly, first to Zachary and then Paul. In unison they each reach forth to touch one of Peter's shoulders and he instantly becomes calm and feels the sense of oneness and joy that they had only recently shared while playing in the light together.

Smiling, and nodding with a gentle knowing, the entity turns and walks forward into the structure, gesturing with a hand over his shoulder for our trio to follow.

Zachary and Paul more or less drag Peter behind them for the first several meters until he regains his composure and is able to move with them on his own. As they flow forward, much moreso than any sense of walking, Peter is in awe of what he sees as the entity comes to a point where he stops and turns, stepping aside.

There, before them, is an ornate chair of great beauty and a vast marvelously long table with a mirror-like finish that seems to continue on almost the entire length of the whole structure. Peter is instantly reminded of the wonderful craftsmanship that he had seen in the benches earlier, and as he looks upon the table, the entity motions him to take a position at the table and to seat himself in the chair.

Swiftly looking to Paul, Paul nods and smiles. Looking next to Zachary, Zachary winks and nods as well.

Peter seats himself and finds to his amazement that, although the chair looks rigid and uncomfortable, as ornate objects on Earth often were, this one is not at all like that. It is as though the chair strives to mold itself to him, to support and cradle him as though it is alive and striving to please him.

With his hands dutifully in his lap, Peter now studies the table more carefully and looks upon its expanse, noting with amazement the depth that is present in the marble or alabaster-like finish. He is awe-struck.

Suddenly, Peter feels a gentle tap upon his shoulder. Looking up, he sees Zachary motioning to his left, where the entity stands with a great book in his arms. In an instant, Peter recognizes it as that which was borne by the female entity and referred to as the Book of Wisdom.

The entity, radiating gentleness and compassionate understanding, and yet all the while exuding this timeless sense of wisdom, now speaks to Peter. "Peter, this book you have seen and wondered upon in recent times contains all there is about you… your potential, your experiences, your hopes, your dreams, your fears, your doubts. Whatever you have been, whatever you shall be, all of your potentials – everything – is represented here."

Reflecting upon the words of the entity, Peter turns to Paul, who is now adjacent to him to his right, and again to Zachary, who is just a bit back and to his left, and sees their smiling faces of reassurance. Looking back up into the eyes of the entity, Peter, somewhat fortified by his recent experience and by the presence of his trusted friends, speaks, asking these things, "Sir, I feel honored to be here and in your presence, and in the company of my dear friends. I know not for what purpose I am here, nor have I knowledge of this book and its content or purpose. I only know somehow inside of me that it is important, and that you, sir, are revered and honored by many. I wish only to express to you the joy that I have within me, and the humbleness I feel at being treated so kindly and so lovingly by all of you," with which he turns once again to look up at Zachary and then over to Paul, receiving from each of them a gentle, smiling nod.

Turning again to the entity with the book, Peter continues, "There is much that I do not understand. I assume since you know most things about me, you probably know that, too. I don't know if everyone who leaves the Earth experiences just what I am experiencing. Though if that is so,

I wish we could know while we are still on Earth that life continues in this wonderful way. It would make things so much easier somehow. But if everyone doesn't get to experience this, I would like to know what others do experience, and what exactly determines who experiences what and where. It is difficult, sir, to be seated here," gesturing across the table and around the very ornate room with a sweep of his hand, "and to be amidst all of this finery, beauty, and perfection. It is... well... difficult for me to understand. Why me? I have a friend. His name is Wilbur, sir. You may not know him, but Zachary does and Paul, too. He is experiencing a realm far less wondrous than this. So, again sir, I ask you, why me? Why not Wilbur?"

At this, the entity, yet holding the book, begins to take on a radiance of incredible brilliance, and the room fills with a golden-white light. And yet, the entity is still visible.

A heaviness, a weariness, a sense of a need for rest, comes upon Peter, and suddenly he feels a hand on each shoulder, one from Paul and one from Zachary.

The entity, still visible to Peter, but glowing brilliantly, speaks. "Peter, you are as you have been described to me. I shall return, and I shall answer your questions. But for now, consider this... you have gained much and you have passed a challenge of your own spirit. Rest now, and we shall be together again before, as you say, the twinkling of an eye."

With which, the swift envelopment of the brilliant lights the trio had experienced, once again envelops them.

And Peter slips into a state of spiritual sleep.

Ask yourselves about what has been given here.

Some of you will know, others will intuit... here are opportunities for you to gain much about the nature of your own spirit—the universe within.

CHAPTER 8

Spiritual Acceptance
OCTOBER 4, 1990

Consider what role habits of familiarity play in your life, as Peter learns how these limit his potential.

He will discover that, rather than sources of alienation, if his joy flows from within, independent of others, differences of opinion become the beautiful contrasts that make up the great tapestry of life, and that through sharing, unfettered by clinging to differences, wondrous growth can follow for all involved.

Peter is a bit groggy and it takes him a moment to recognize that Paul is present, as is Zachary. He looks back and forth from one to the other, and it is Zachary's warm smile and impish way of grinning that sort of breaks the ice.

"Quite an experience, eh, Pete?"

There is a pause before Peter responds. "It was that, and much more, as I guess you could discern."

"I discerned it all right. I could even feel it, from the top of my being to the bottom. Quite an entity, that one, wouldn't you say, Pete?"

"Yes, and there was something… well I can't quite put my finger on it, but it seems as though I've seen him before."

Peter is still looking at Paul, as though to invite him into the conversation, almost as though he's pleading with Paul to come forth with answers. Still smiling, Paul simply gazes as Zachary answers, "Well, it's hard to say, Pete. Most of us have been around a few times. Who knows how many entities we've seen here and there, and probably seen some of them more than once. Know what I mean?"

With that, Peter turns to look back at Zachary, who is now studying Peter's countenance carefully. Peter responds, "Wait a minute, now. You're talking about that reincarnation stuff, aren't you? I know a bit about it. I guess this is as good a time as any to ask about it. Is that alright?"

"Sure. Ask away."

"Well, is it true? I mean, do we come and go, sort of like a revolving door, into and out of the Earth realm? And if it's true, what's behind it all, anyway? Once I've been here, why would I want to go back there? Would I have to go back? If I did want to go back there, would I always come here? I don't remember being here before. Have I been? Do others come here? Why are you here? Enough questions, Zack?"

Nodding vigorously, Zachary looks down and states, "Quite enough, thanks. I wouldn't want to overwork Paul, you see."

A small chuckle can be heard from Zachary as he then looks up squarely at Paul, who simply nods and warmly turns to Peter. "Well, Peter, reincarnation is a fact for some and an illusion for others. What I mean by that is some entities do, indeed, go into and out of the Earth realm and even other places, like you said, as though there were a revolving door. For some of them it's not actually much different from that description. But in the more specific sense, yes, you have been in the Earth realm a number of times previous to this just-previous experience, and if you think about it hard enough, you'll remember them. In fact, you may recall we've spoken of it in the past."

Peter reaches into his consciousness to grasp specifically what Paul is speaking of.

Paul continues, "To answer another of your other questions, yes, other entities do come and go here. Some of them, you might say, with regularity, others only once or twice, and yet others come here and stay awhile. It's really their choice and is dependent somewhat upon what they want in terms of their own... let me just call it objectives, to make it clearer to you.

"In the word 'objectives' let me add several new concepts for you. An objective can be, for example in the Earth realm, dreaming about, planning for, saving for, a new automobile and then someday it becomes a reality. Here, an objective might be to regain something that you already have. An example of this would be some bit of knowledge, or some talent you may have developed earlier and have subsequently forgotten, due to a lack of application or use of it."

Studying Paul carefully, Peter nods subtly, indicating he has grasped what has been said but also that he has not understood to the fullest extent. All the while Paul is speaking, Peter is continuing to search his memories to find the references of his past, as Paul has spoken of.

Paul pauses a moment, and Zachary takes over. "You see, Pete, what Paul's telling you is that some folks like certain things and get stuck to them, and no matter how hard they try to let go of them, those things stick tight. On Earth, they are called habits, or obsessions. Not a big deal, mind you, but they need to be dealt with, reckoned with, and in order to reckon with them, they keep going back to work on them. They chip away a bit here, a bit there. Finally one day, bang... they've got it, and they can let go if they want to. Now that they have the capacity to let go, they don't have to, because it's no longer an obstacle, an impediment to them—it's simply a matter of choice. Get the difference?"

This time, Peter nods vigorously. "Yep, I see that, alright. It's clear as a bell. Sorry, Paul, I just couldn't grasp what you were saying, but with the little addendum Zack added there, I get it very well. Continue on, will you, Paul? This is very interesting."

Nodding at Zachary to thank him for his assistance, Paul turns back to Peter and continues. "So, if you've got that, Peter, now think of it in terms of having been to other places other than the Earth. For example, you're now in this place that we've come to call The Garden, and you've been to the other place where Wilbur dwells, which we have come to call The Crystal Workers Realm. You now have been to Wilbur's realm sufficient times so as to be capable of going there and coming back, essentially on your own."

"Wait a minute," Peter interrupts. "I don't think I'm ready for that yet. I mean I don't even know how we got there. It was all too quick, and every time I go there I seem to get tired real quick. You guys know that. More than once you've had to pick me up and almost drag me back here."

Zachary slaps his thigh and laughs aloud, creating all sorts of jangling and bright dancing lights about them, typical of the Realm of Light in which they are currently resting.

Noting the lights and the brilliance around him again for a moment, caused by Zachary's laughter, Peter is suddenly calmed, as though the lights and the sounds, the energies, all pass through him, cleansing him. "Thanks, Zack. As they say on Earth, I needed that."

"Well, look, here's the deal... you could go to Wilbur's realm on your own if you wanted to."

There is a long pause as Peter contemplates this as a real possibility, knowing that Zachary would never mislead him. As he studies Zachary, he realizes that, in fact, he could travel on his own, but also that the presence of Paul and Zachary and the reassurance that comes along with that makes the trip to Wilbur's realm easier and more pleasant.

Zachary responds to Peter's thoughts, "See, I told you. You know you can. It's just that you are familiar with only one way of doing it, and that familiarity has become such in this short number of experiences that you prefer it to claiming your own ability. Isn't that an amazing discovery, Pete?"

Peter pauses a moment, looking from Paul to Zachary. "Well, I guess it is. It's not a discovery I was looking for, but you're right. I am amazed at that. I guess it says something about me."

"It says something about all of us, doesn't it, Zachary?" adds Paul.

"Oh my, yes. You know me. I can be as stuck in a rut as the best of them."

All three laugh at this, and cascading lights inundate them. As each little sphere of light bumps against one of them, a sound is created, so that each of them has light dancing over and within them, changing hues and patterns swirling this way and that.

It is Paul, who finally raises a hand and calms the other two. "You know, Peter, there really is a lot to what Zachary is saying. We are in a rut. You might joke about it, but only because you don't consciously know that much about Zachary and me yet."

Quickly tensing, Peter responds very strongly, "I know all I need to know about you two, Paul. I know you are good. I know you are trustworthy… the kindest, warmest people I have ever met in all of my existences, wherever they might have been and whoever or whatever I might have been. So, don't for a moment, try to tell me that you have any shortcomings, because I won't hear of it."

With that, Zachary bursts into laughter again.

Turning to look sternly at Zachary, Peter is melted by the warmth and compassion of his gaze, even though Zachary continues to laugh heartily. Instantly, Peter is swept up in this again, and finds himself laughing at his own defensiveness of these, the very people to whom he is speaking.

Finally, Paul says, "We thank you for that, Peter, but I did mean what I said. Each of us in these realms is, in a way, interdependent upon the other. When you are joyful, I am joyful. When I am joyful, Zachary is joyful."

With that, Zachary interjects, "Wait a minute. I thought I was always joyful. You mean my joy is dependent upon your joy, and Peter's joy?"

"You know that is so, Zachary. Let's stop joking with Peter for a moment and help him understand this concept. What do you say?"

Zachary straightens himself and answers, "You're right, Paul. Sorry if I deterred you. Do continue. I think he's ready, and I think it's time."

Paul turns back to Peter, who is visibly shaken by this little exchange between his friends, for he has evaluated the exchange as though it were a confrontation, and this has had an impact upon him.

Paul, studying Peter carefully, asks, "Are you well?"

Softly, Peter responds, "Yes, I believe so."

"Would you care to discuss what you are feeling?"

"Well, I don't really know how to tell you what I am feeling, but then, you probably already know anyway."

"We do, but it is important for you to express it. Could you try?"

"Well, it's just that the two of you have been so very important to me and to my joy here, and I have always thought of the two of you as..." pausing for a prolonged period of time, Peter continues, "well, perfect... as something I wanted to be. I had thought of each of you as unquestionably fond and loving to one another. So what I just heard shook me up. It brought to mind some memories from Earth. When people on Earth don't agree, they seem to transform that disagreement into something that alienates them from one another. It's hard to describe. They can't accept the fact that one might see something one way and the other yet another way, and still be friends. It's like the difference of perspective creates a barrier between them. Sometimes they even become enemies simply because they each see the same thing differently. I know I haven't expressed this very well, but it's the best I can do. I hope it's what you're looking for, Paul."

Paul responds gently but with a note of seriousness, "I believe it is what I was looking for, Peter, but you see... I didn't know what your answer would be."

Peter is startled by Paul's comment, and only after some passage of time is he able to converse again. "Wait a minute. You've always known what my thoughts were. You've even communicated with me without speaking. I guess I just thought that you knew everything. Now you're telling me you don't? Now you're telling me... well... what exactly are you telling me? This is becoming much less pleasant for me. I don't understand. Am I making something out of nothing here? What's happening to us?"

Paul and Zachary exchange nods, and then each extends an arm around Peter and another around each other. Peter slowly raises his arms to interlock his with each of them, and again they have formed their triad. Ever so slowly the light begins to intensify. Only now does Peter realize that the brilliance of their light had dimmed dramatically.

As they continue with linked arms to look from one to the other, Zachary's gaze catches Peter's eyes, and Peter, in the midst of some seriousness now, receives from Zachary, a wink, and these comments, "No big deal, Pete. Let's not get tense here. Spoil the whole day. We're on an outing, you know. Let's have some fun."

Peter can feel an electricity flowing from Zachary, inundating him, cascading all over his being, and then from Paul, the same. It amplifies, as though two different tones are converging to form a chord, a harmonic. Swirling up from them, it bursts overhead in an aerial fireworks-like display of lights that stream down around them.

Zachary chuckles. Then, looking at Peter, he begins to laugh aloud. "You look like one of those wooden Indians on Earth standing in front of a cigar store, Pete. Loosen up."

In that moment, the image of what Zachary described, literally appears, and Peter begins to laugh, as does Paul.

"Wait a minute," retorts Zachary, "that's unfair. Let's make that three wooden Indians." As two more wooden Indians appear, they begin to laugh even louder.

Peter jokes, "This one looks like Zack. No, wait a minute... it's Paul. That's Zack over there."

Their humor mounts, and upward they go, spiraling and tumbling. They continue this, joyously, for a considerable measure of time. As they finally come to rest, Peter's luminosity is brilliant once again.

Paul resumes with, "Let me explain all this to you, Peter, to be certain that you fully understand. As you can sense, it is important. What Zachary and I are trying to point out to you is that you must look to none of us as being greater than you, and for that matter, you must not look at Wilbur as being lesser than we. Before you answer and defend yourself, we know that you don't look upon him as lesser, but you do look upon his plight in a way that brings about an attitude suggesting limitation, and that is what I'm speaking of.

"When I told you I didn't really know what you were thinking or feeling, it is because although I know it, I cannot truly feel it. I cannot define it. I know of the conflict between people in the Earth realm, but you have just returned from there. You have seen it. You have lived it recently. You know of it, then, in a way that I cannot, and it is that which I sought from you.

"The exchange between Zachary and me was not what you think. It has naught to do with the nature of things in the realm of Earth, but rather, was given intentionally as a triggering mechanism to bring forth this certain reality from you, this certain consciousness.

"Now, do not think that we have used this triggering mechanism as trickery. We did not. To a degree, Zachary and I do differ in our perspectives, in our ideals, our goals, and purposes. Zachary chooses to work in one way, and I choose to work in another. Where we can, we work together, and where we find that our intents and purposes lead us in differing ways, then we honor that. We can discuss our differences, and we grow as we do. We do not find fault nor hatred in difference. To the contrary, we find beauty and joy in the differences... the wondrous uniqueness of each of us, here, in the Earth realm, and in every realm."

Obviously relieved by this, Peter now responds, more balanced, "I think I understand. What you have shown me is that Zachary can think and do one thing, and you another, and in spite of those differences, you can still love one another and be the best of friends. Is that what you are saying?"

"Precisely, Peter, and it is even much more than that, much deeper and much more eternal than you could comprehend in the moment. Zachary has great abilities, and as stated to you previously, he hasn't come by them idly, or by chance. In other words, they aren't just idle gifts showered on him that I don't have. They are, rather, the result of choices, pathways that predicated these abilities. Once again, this is rather like people in the realm of Earth who possess an interest, or a talent, and work at it. For example, pianists practice, discipline and devote themselves, and they become accomplished. Perhaps they even perform for others, becoming notable. True?"

"That is true, but exactly what is it you are trying to help me see here?"

"Well, just this, Peter... we can assume that because they are very practiced in their particular talent, that well-developed talent is what makes them great... that which makes them famous or uniquely respected. Would you say that is a true statement regarding Earth?"

"Sounds right to me."

"At what point of development and dedication is it that one's 'special-ness' begins to show? In other words, if I like music and I live in the Earth realm, and I practice the piano daily and become moderately good, am I then considered moderately special? Moderately famous?"

Peter thinks about this and then answers, "Well, that's not quite the way it works, Paul. It seems like on Earth you're either famous or you're not. You are accomplished and respected or you're not. I don't think there is such a thing as being half-famous," With which they all roll about, laughing.

"Let's see how I can explain it to you," continues Peter. "You do get recognition as you begin the process of development, and that recognition comes in bits and pieces. But I'll tell you something... very often on Earth, it's the breaks that are important. If the right person hears you at the right time and you sound promising, you'll be supported and encouraged. You'll be given opportunities that a person who isn't heard at the right time and place won't get."

Looking from Peter then over to Zachary, Paul nods.

"Well, Pete," begins Zachary, picking up the conversation, "that sounds like a rather poorly balanced system, doesn't it? I mean, why would two or three people all at the same stage of development not get the same recognition, the same treatment? For example, how would it be if one of them is, by Earthly standards, pleasant to look at, and the other ones aren't? Would he or she be favored?"

"Oh, yes, indeed," answers Peter. "Looks are very important on Earth. That is, unless the talent is exceptional. Then it doesn't matter what you look like. Then it sort of turns about and goes the other way... the more accomplished, the less important the appearance is."

"Interesting," answers Zachary. "Do you know the point at which that begins to swing and go the other way?"

"Well, I hadn't thought about it in that sense before. I wouldn't know how to measure something like that."

"That's all right, Pete, we appreciate the information you are giving. Here's the point to our questioning... here in these realms, all entities are considered for their accomplishments in terms of something that we call their 'spiritual acceptance,' their ability to accept their spiritual potential. Don't let the term 'spiritual acceptance' throw you. What it means is, we look at entities as having attained the level of their own willingness. In other words, it's as high as they are willing to go at that point. So, we can look at a certain point of willingness and see everyone who's at that point, and we would treat all those entities one and the same, regardless of any other factor. Does that make sense?"

"I think it does. Somehow, deep within, I know what you're saying. I don't have a complete handle on it, but I think I've got the main point. So, again, what's this all about, anyway? I'm still not clear what you are trying to teach me."

"We aren't really teaching you," Zachary explains further. "We're re-awakening. We're sharing. We're all learning here. We don't want you to think of us as the teachers and yourself as the student. Let's just think of ourselves as friends, each with different perspectives, different talents, and we've come together to share them."

"Good, Zachary. I like that. It has a nice feel to it, and I can accept that. Even though I don't much feel I am quite your equal here, I can accept it, because I know the spirit in which you are suggesting it."

Zachary, looking squarely at Peter, answers, "It is true, though, Peter. Plain and simple. You're thinking of yourself as a newcomer here, but you aren't actually new in that sense; you're simply reawakened to this realm. But that's enough on that. Let's turn to something else. We just wanted to get that set as a foundation for you before we meet our new friend again. We wouldn't have completed our work as we had promised him, if we hadn't cleared some of this up."

Staring at Zachary, Peter asks, "Does that comment mean you know this man... this entity, as you call him?"

"Oh, sure, Pete. We know him quite well, in fact."

"Well, would you mind answering some questions?"

"Of course. Go ahead."

"Who is this entity, and where does he come from? Why does he have the sense of familiarity to me that he does? Why does he seem so similar to the females that were here? The ladies? And it just dawned on me, you told me that the one female entity was the keeper of that book, or my book, or whatever it is. Now, how is it that this man has it?" looking at that point from Zachary to Paul and again.

"Hey, Pete, those are great questions. Now look, it's this way... the man, as we've come to call him, is the same entity as the woman you saw earlier who had the book."

With that, Peter visibly illuminates, and his light begins to crackle. Simultaneously, Paul and Zachary each swiftly reach out to touch one of his shoulders.

Slowly, the crackling subsides and Peter is brought back to a state of balance. "What are you telling me, Zack? That man and that woman are the same? What is this, some sort of costume and make-up thing, like in the theater?"

A bit wary of the impact on Peter because of his previous comment, Zachary continues softly, "What I'm saying is that they are, in fact, one and the same entity. Remember now, you're not in physical body. Don't forget that for a moment as we continue this conversation or we'll lose you and have to wait again until you rebalance. Okay?"

Nervously, Peter responds, "I'll try my best. Just take it slow, please. This is very unsettling to me."

"Okay. I'll... go... very... slow. You... tell... me..."

Breaking out in laughter, Peter interrupts, "No, Zack. You know very well what I mean. Uh... but thanks for the little bit of lifting laughter. I feel better. Go ahead now."

With that, Zachary smiles and nods, and Paul also nods warmly to Zachary, as though to say, "Well done."

Zachary continues. "You're bringing too much of your Earthly thinking into play here, if you'll forgive me.

That's not a criticism. It's expected. After all, you've got a lot of that left over, and it's valuable… we don't want you to lose it or throw it away. But we do want you to have both perspectives, so here is the answer to your question…

"The entity in question you last saw as a male entity in the Great Hall, as we call it, is free, unlimited. In other words, his spiritual acceptance – or hers, depending on where you see them – is sufficient that such things are no longer a limitation. In fact, the entity has had physical forms both of male and female in differing experiences… we'll call them incarnations… where they are in physical form or finite body. As such, it's a simple matter for that entity to use whichever of these might be the more appropriate in the situation.

"In the first meeting, the entity chose the female, and brought along a friend for polarity… balance. You know, plus-minus… too many males and no females. Not that the physical body is the complete indicator of that. It's the energy within same, not the body. The body is the symbol of that polarity, just as in the Earth, only here, it's reduced more or refined more to a purer state. And that physical being was for the purpose of continuity and for comprehension and understanding. Your acceptance level would have been shattered had they been expressed in some other more infinite form. See? How's that? Still with me?"

"Yep, I'm with you, Zack. Step by step, I'm grasping it. I don't understand it all, but I'm starting to get the picture here. So you're saying that when we leave the Earth, when we 'die,' we can have any form? Is that what you're saying?"

"That's great, Pete. That's what I'm saying. There are some factors that come in to play here. They largely have to do with one's level of acceptance, one's ability to perceive and to accept. Remember, I stated to you previously 'first will and then action'? The will has to do with the conception and ability to allow something to be; the action comes into focus here by actually doing it, being it, or enacting it. In other words, making blueprints and then building something from them. The blueprint stage is the will, and the building part of it... that's the action. Simple, eh?"

"Well, I guess. At least it's conceptually simple. But how about doing it? Is that also just as straightforward?"

"It sure is. In fact, you've done it a number of times and haven't even realized it."

"I have? When? Name one time."

"Well, let's see. You did it at one point when we passed from the Garden Realm to Wilbur's. You did it another time when we went back, and another time when..."

"Wait a minute," Peter interrupts. "I don't remember doing anything except hanging onto the two of you when we went from the Garden to Wilbur's realm. Point out to me what I did and how I did it."

"Sure thing, Pete. I asked you if you would like to take a trip with me, a little journey. Remember?"

"Well, yes, sure. I remember that."

"And I asked Paul if he'd like to come along?"

"Yes, I remember you asking Paul."

"Okay, well that's the blueprint."

"You're kidding. That's it? You ask and I say yes, and that's the blueprint?"

"In a manner of speaking, that's it," responds Paul, interjecting. "What Zachary is saying to you is, it is not complicated. If you want it to be, it can be. It can be as complex as you need it to be. The complexity comes about through the process of attempting to understand and grasp something in the finite definition carried over from the Earth. Here, however, and also on Earth if one would reach that level of acceptance there, you have only to conceptualize it, and you have the blueprint. Then you have only to go forward into that conception to actualize it."

"Okay, just a minute here. Let me get this straight. Zack here asks me to go on a trip. I say yes, and so I've created the opportunity for something to be built?"

"That's in essence true, Peter," answers Paul.

"And then this action part, that Zack keeps talking about, that's what you called, 'going into that concept'?"

"That is correct," responds Paul once again. "Let me help you here a bit, if I might. By 'going into it,' I'm saying the same thing as Zachary is when he says 'take action.' Again, this is simply the difference, as we spoke of, between our perceptions—Zachary is all for what he calls action... forthrightness, confidence, boldness, going forward. And I admire that sincerely and deeply in him. As a matter of fact, I love it in him. He's a wonder."

With which, Zachary looks down and states softly, "Well, thank you, Paul. Nice of you. Thank you."

Paul smiles. "As you know, Zachary, I mean it."

Zachary does not respond.

Paul turns to Peter and continues, "My comment or perspective is simply that you create something in the sense of an image, a blueprint, a pattern, and then you go into that, bring it in or onto yourself by becoming a part of it. It's sort of like thinking of a song in your mind and then audibly trying to hum it. Like thinking of a picture in your mind and then attempting to place that picture on canvas. See?"

Peter pauses, looks down, and then up at each of them, and finally states, "I think I am beginning to grasp this. What I feel you are trying to tell me is that, as much as I am willing to allow myself to think of something, then that's the extent to which it can actually be?"

"Hey, good, Pete. That's excellent! You hit it right, square on the center. Let's hear some more."

"Okay, Zack. Let me see then. I've thought of it, and now I have to do something with that thought. I would need to strengthen that thought, wouldn't I?"

"Good," answers Paul.

"Excellent," responds Zachary.

"Strengthen it. Let's see," ponders Peter. "How does one strengthen a thought?"

"Easy," answers Zachary. "Think butterflies, and you've got butterflies. Think flowers, and you've got flowers. Will, followed by action."

Paul, nods a smile to Zachary, then turns to Peter and states, "And I would add to that which Zachary has given, think of butterflies, and reach out and be a butterfly... be a part of that thought. Image in your mind, in your being, the dimensions, the patterns, the shapes. Image and remember and create the flight of a butterfly. That is the counterpart to Zachary's action. Understand?"

"The butterfly always existed in the mind of God, awaiting someone, such as you, Peter, to conceive of it," Zachary explains further. "Once you do that, in these realms, you actually give life to the butterfly. From that point forward, the butterfly exists, every bit as real as you and I. Even if you were to begin to doubt it, as you did the flowers, it still exists... you simply wouldn't be able to perceive it."

"Well, thank you both," Peter responds. "I believe I understand what you're trying to tell me."

"Good, because we have a meeting soon. Are you feeling well enough now to return?"

"To where?" asks Peter.

"To the Great Hall. Remember?"

"Oh, my goodness, yes. I forgot for a moment there. How could I forget that?"

Paul chuckles a bit and states, "That's not difficult at all. Forgetting is easy. It's remembering that's hard."

They all laugh and the lights and sounds cascade again, but this time they are strangely subdued - soft, gentle - and Peter hears a wonderful sound, as though someone has struck a giant bell somewhere off in the distance.

A golden-white light slowly begins to envelop them, and as it does, Peter can feel himself moving swiftly. He feels his arms clasped by those of Paul and Zachary, and in the next instant he is before the table in the Great Hall.

On the other side of the table is a concentration of the golden-white light Peter had seen before. He stands awestruck by its brilliance and luminosity, and the incredible warmth and wondrous feeling that it imparts to him, as fingers of light reach out and penetrate his being. He is transfixed, peering into the center of the orb of light and begins to see a figure taking shape. Instantly, he recognizes the outline as the entity of Wisdom. Finally the figure appears fully and clearly, though still shrouded in the golden orb of light. Embraced in his left arm is the great book.

With his eyes directly upon Peter, he nods softly, a warmth and radiance coming from him, as though he had smiled broadly, but Peter can see no change in his facial expressions, only his eyes meeting his own. The entity gestures again for Peter to sit in the great ornate chair. As Peter does, he looks to his right and left to find with delight that he is flanked on the left and right by Zachary and Paul.

All three turn to look at the figure, who stands before them across the table. "You have done well, good friends, and we are pleased at your progress. Have you questions that you would wish to continue with here, Peter? Or shall I speak?"

Sensing the greater wisdom, Peter responds, "I should prefer, sir, that you would speak. I am certain that you know of what lies in my heart and what questions I have. I am confident that you shall address any of those as you know to be the better for me, and of course for my dear friends here, Zachary," and he turns to look upon each one as he names them, "and Paul."

"Well chosen, my friend, and it is indeed so. You have learned much recently, and you have accomplished much, to the credit of yourself and your dear companions," and he nods to each of them in turn. "We should like the nature of this meeting to be primarily dedicated to the answering of your questions as you had expressed them to us in our last meeting. Is this acceptable to you, Peter?"

Peter, awed by the fact that this entity of obvious wisdom and majesty would ask for his permission, finds difficulty in answering. "It is indeed very acceptable, sir, and welcomed." Hearing his own voice, he finds with interest that his speech and manner seem different each time he is before this entity. He wonders at this. What power has this entity to transform him? As he looks carefully from Zachary to Paul, it is evident that the entity has a similar impact upon them as well. He turns to focus again on the entity, who is obviously, he notes, awaiting the conclusion of his thoughts.

"I apologize, sir. Please do continue."

With which, the entity answers, "No apology is needed here, Peter. That is always true. Previously, you spoke the words, 'Why me?' and you also in your commentary made a reference to the entity, Wilbur. Do you recall this?"

"Yes, sir, I do," answers Peter.

"We are pleased that in our last meeting, your concern was for another whose plight, as you saw it, was less than your own. You may recall that we mentioned to you that you had passed a challenge of your own spirit. This was meant, and intentionally so, that you would understand that this is an accomplishment of significance," and the entity pauses, gazing across the table gently at Peter.

Awkward in the moment of silence, Peter feels he should respond. "Sir, I am flattered and honored at your comments. I do not in this moment understand how I exemplified anything extraordinary in that action, nor do I understand why you consider those statements I gave to be something which is beyond the norm. Yet, sir, if you say it is so, I do accept this, for I feel in my heart that you are wise, and that you would speak to me only truth."

The entity spreads the essence of a smile across the table to cascade down over Peter. Yet again, only his eyes show this. His face is blissful, but not indicating the smile. It is his eyes that smile across the table to Peter, as though the true entity were present in the eyes, and the body merely a container for the eyes to dwell in. "We had asked Zachary earlier," the entity continues on, "if he would help you to develop a relationship with Wilbur, for Wilbur is at a point wherein he can grow. You might understand this better in your own examples the three of you were discussing. At what point does an entity become considered famous or excellent or ready?"

Somewhat startled that the entity obviously knew and thus had heard or seen all that transpired, Peter responds a bit nervously, "I comprehend your statement, and accept it. But I know not of these things... of how I might possibly be a help to Wilbur in his personal growth. Can I be trained or guided, that I might do what it is that you are asking me to do? Can it be that Zachary and Paul might assist me in this, sir?"

The entity looks from one to the other, and as he does, each of them bows just slightly at his gaze. "As you wish, Peter. They have accepted your invitation and will help you. But understand that you are, in and of yourself, capable of serving this call, else it would not have been offered to you. In fact, both Zachary and Paul consider it to be an honor and a privilege to be permitted to accompany you, and to assist you in that work. Do you understand this, Peter?"

"I think so, sir. However, once again, I do not understand why you have chosen me, nor do I understand why they, my friends, would consider it an honor to serve with me. It seems it would be more appropriate for me to serve with them. No disrespect intended, sir, but that is truly what is in my heart and in my thoughts."

"We have heard your words, and we accept your thoughts and compliment you for them. In times ahead, you will come to understand why it is that you have been chosen. For now, we shall transfer, in effect, certain opportunities to you and your group that these works might be presented before Wilbur. You will find a helpmeet to this work present in Wilbur's realm. In the form of his expression at present, you know of him as David. He is one of our group and is present there for the purpose of assisting. Should you ever have a need or that which you are in want for, you are encouraged to ask of David and he will attend to that need, whatsoe'er it might be. Do you understand this?"

Peter responds, somewhat startled, but yet with a sense of knowing within, that David was too wonderful, too beautiful, too special, to be just a crystal worker. As he has this thought, he knows instantly the error in it, for he recalls the comments between Zachary and Paul and himself. With that he looks up at the entity across the table from him and states, "Please forgive me for that thought, sir. It is, I guess I might say, out of habit. I recognize the error of it and I do apologize."

The entity once again radiates a smile of warmth from his eyes. "Remember, Peter, you needn't apologize here, but we accept your statement, and so now we shall depart again. As we do, know that we are always near at hand. Should there be the need, you have only but to call." Without waiting for a response, the entity's outline begins to fade, and the orb of light moves back to its earlier position and becomes just that, once again—a radiant, brilliant light.

In that instant, Peter, Paul, and Zachary, fall into the light and move into a state of spiritual rest.

Experiences learned and applied are always worthy of recognition, and become gifts to others when shared.

CHAPTER 9

Oneness
NOVEMBER 10, 1990

Peter, Paul and Zachary journeyed a great deal during their spiritual rest. They revisited many of Peter's past experiences, both incarnative and other experiences not involving physical form ... some shared by the three of them, and some experiences moreso as individuals.

Of particular note and importance here is the fact that they have also viewed much of Wilbur's past experiences. They have looked upon his involvements with the Earth - his needs and his wants - to the extent that Peter now knows Wilbur quite well, for example much as you might experience having known someone since early childhood. Peter now knows Wilbur to this depth and breadth, and he understands much more the nature of Wilbur's present position and as such, can comprehend where he's at (in your colloquial terminology of the Earth). So, in the Earth-time that has transpired, very much has been accomplished.

Peter continues his questions with his colleagues Zachary and Paul. These discussions provide him with insights, which he will rely upon in times ahead when they offer their help to Wilbur.

The trio is gathered once again at their favorite spot on the high knoll of green, lush expanse in what has come to be called Peter's Garden.

"Well, Peter," begins Paul, "what are your thoughts at this point? That is, if you have any?"

Zachary chuckles. "You must be joking, Paul. Pete hasn't been without a question since we met. Right, Pete?"

Inspired and somewhat grateful for Zachary's interjection of lightness, Peter answers, "Yes, I guess that's so. Even in what we've just reviewed, I still seem to have more questions than I have answers. And with all that we have learned and all that I now know about myself, each of you, and Wilbur, it's almost like with each answer I get, two or three new questions pop up. It's incredible. I can't imagine where it will ever end. Is it always like this?" Turning to look first at Zachary and then at Paul, Peter pauses.

Paul steps forward, "Look at it this way, Peter. When you're considering infinity and eternity, doesn't it seem logical that with each new bit of knowledge, multiple new areas of awareness are sure to come forward? And as each new area of awareness comes forward, it is natural to have questions about each of those. So it is sort of like an inverted pyramid, like we've talked about before. The focal point of that pyramid is the here and now, and the next level is tomorrow and beyond that is the next week (which is now seven individual blocks) and the next month which has thirty or thirty-one, as you might recall it from on Earth (except for that odd month), and so forth. Do you see, Peter?"

"Yes, I can visualize that. Well, listen, even though we've got all this information now that you have graciously helped me to gather about myself, I need to ask some questions here about an area that really has me puzzled. Why is it that I don't feel, uh… you know, sadness or emotional bonds to my family? I remember when we went through the… records, I think you called them, there were a few moments here and there where I felt a tug at some level of my being, but not like I would when I was on Earth. There would be times there when I'd be off on a business trip, and I'd miss my family a lot. Couldn't be gone for two consecutive days without calling them three or four times just to hear their voices. And here I am now... you know... uh... dead."

Zachary bursts into uproarious laughter. Paul, having difficulty containing his chuckles, looks down and fidgets with the earth and flowers and grass. Then Peter, caught in their humor, also bursts out laughing. Once again, colors and sounds cascade down as though they were being sprinkled upon the group from a giant shaker of some sort; spontaneous bursts of color and light, all of which are interwoven with a melodious sound. This, as always in the past, seems to ease what was approaching a rather tense moment.

Peter, composing himself, continues on, "Well, I guess you know what I mean. I don't have my physical body any more. However it is that I appear to you and others now, this outer expression of me never seems to be hungry, never seems to be thirsty, is never cold nor warm to a significant degree. I don't have difficulty with that concept, at this point anyway, but why don't I feel the sadness? Why don't I miss my loved ones, like I did on those business weekends?"

There is a long pause, before Zachary is the first to connect with Peter's eyes. As he does, he winks with exaggeration and states, "Obviously, we don't have the answer to that, Pete. Why don't you tell us?"

Somewhat taken aback by that comment, Peter stops to reflect. As he does, his cloak brightens in luminosity, but this time it does not crackle and pop. It is a very controlled, very orderly illumination, as though one were turning an electrical dimmer switch up to increase the current. As this occurs, he feels strangely wonderful. Within this now glowing orb that is his spiritual cloak, Peter seems capable of reason beyond the norm. It is as though he can reach out and grasp a flow of wisdom which, though always present, is strangely more accessible now as he turns within himself, enveloped in the warm radiant glow of his own cloak.

With the passage of several moments, Peter's cloak returns to a normal radiance, and he responds, "Very well,

Zack. I have found my own answer. Thank you. It's quite simple, actually… Inwardly, somewhere within me, I know that they all are well, and that they are attending to their individual needs and purposes, just as I am and you and Paul are. They are in, what I would call, a sort of divine order. The little challenges, or even hardships or pain that they might endure, are steps that they have chosen of their own volition, needed to enhance their awareness and contribute to the ultimate emergence of their greater being."

As Peter completes his explanation, Zachary leaps to his feet, beams a broad smile at him and begins to applaud. Paul responds in kind, so that they are now standing one at either side of Peter, applauding and smiling down at him, who is still seated upon the green expanse.

Somewhat embarrassed by his friends' antics, he calls out over their exuberance, "Come on, guys, it wasn't that significant. And anyway, I'm sure you knew very well what I'd say and how I'd say it," with which both of them pause, looking from one to the other.

It is Paul who answers, "Well, certainly we were aware of the answer, for it is universal knowledge. But what we did not know, Peter, was how you yourself would phrase it. Our enthusiasm is for how you interpreted universal knowledge and brought it forth as a thought-form from the uniqueness of your own being."

Zachary and Paul each extend a hand to Peter and swiftly lift him to an upright position. Zachary brushes Peter off, as he has come to do frequently. Peter looks around at himself and asks, "Have I soiled your cloak here, Zack?"

"Not to worry, Pete," Zachary answers, still brushing him off here and there. "Nothing I can't repair. Just want you to look spiffy. Wouldn't want it to be said of our realm that we had any shoddy dressers here," and they all laugh merrily.

"Okay," comments Peter finally, after a long pause of silence. "I know the two of you are up to something, and that something lies just ahead. But, please, this time, before we go forward and I find myself dunked in up to my eyebrows in new experiences, could you spare me a moment and allow me to ask some questions?"

Swiftly, each of them grasps one of Peter's arms and moves him along towards the benches as Zachary answers, "Pete, you have as much time here as you could ever need, and we'd be glad to answer all the questions that you have, although surely you are beginning to realize that you have the answers within you. But if you would like us to express them to you, as a sort of demonstration or whatnot, we'd certainly always be happy to do that for you."

They each sit on one of the ornate marble benches, which are in a small semi-circle.

Peter resumes. "The entity of the wonderful light that we see in the hall, or... the beautiful structure over there," casting an eye towards its luminosity, down the knoll and over on a second knoll just a distance away. "Who is he?"

"Well, Peter, "Paul responds, "that is indeed a complex question to answer, for he, you see, is not actually a 'he', as you probably have surmised, and as has been somewhat indicated to you. He is not confined to a sexual expression as 'she' or 'he', but rather has unified the completeness of expressions into a singular state of being. After which, that singular state of being, now in its unified state, more or less enjoined itself with other similar souls to become a group or group consciousness. The nature of that group consciousness is one which can easily move from realm to realm, dwell in harmony, adopt other forms, represent itself or himself or herself, as need be, and totally adopt the structure, the confines, the... ideology, of that realm. See?"

"Very well, I understand all that," answers Peter. "But please, who is he and *what* is he if he's not a 'who'? Where does he come from? And what's with the light? And his eyes smiled and communicated with me, and yet I saw no visible smile, just that continual, beautiful radiance and the wonderful, blissful appearance on his face. What is the source of that power, that light or love?"

Paul continues with, "The same source that's within each of us, in him... or them, is unburdened, unbridled, unlimited. As such, it can be controlled at will, directed in accordance with the need or desire. That is the source. If you are looking for a name or a title, as your questions clearly indicate, Peter, we would have to offer to you that the power – the source – is God."

In that moment, Peter recognizes something very unique happening within him. As he does, Zachary and Paul simply observe Peter's reactions. This time, there is only the slightest hint of random electrical-like currents bouncing around on his cloak. The sparkling and popping that evidences Peter's attempt to spiritually and mentally digest that comment is now very subtle.

Zachary reaches out and touches Peter's shoulder. "Let's talk about it, Pete. Don't try to digest all that in one swallow. That's a big mouthful... big enough for any of us to have some difficulty with. Paul and I have learned to hold some things in a state of continual reference, adding a bit here and there, building a thought-form, a consciousness, building a foundation, but doing it bit by bit, step by step. You know, Pete, it's like on Earth. If you have a nice tasty meal in front of you, you can't very well consume it all in one bite. So you use a cutting utensil and you eat it piece by piece. Why not approach this whole issue in a similar manner?"

Peter visibly calms himself. "Good advice. I accept it, Zack, and I thank you, Paul, for your answer to my question. Would it be alright if I continue on with my next question?"

"Please do," answers Paul.

Zachary simply nods, and as Peter pauses to gather his thoughts, Zachary states, barely audible, "This ought to be a good one."

Peter swiftly turns to Zachary, smiling broadly. "I think it is, Zack. I think it is. I want to talk to you some more about this cloak you've given me. I know that Paul has already helped me with this somewhat, but now that I have had a longer time to wear it, I have more questions. Why am I different when I'm wearing your cloak? What are you giving me in the form of this cloak? It appears in many respects to be like the garments on Earth, and yet, we all know it's not. It's a living thing. It's alive. Yet it's tangible and has substance. Where does it come from? How is it made?"

Peter pauses momentarily for a response, but when none is given, he continues, "Why did you give me your cloak, Zack? Why didn't you give me one, Paul? Or, for that matter, why didn't our 'golden friend' if you'll forgive that reference, for I have no other name by which to call him."

Zachary, leaning back, straightening himself, looking down, fussing over his own cloak, answers, "Not a problem, Pete. Be glad to answer all of your questions. But, as always," looking up, tilting his head with an exaggerated wink, "wouldn't you rather *do* than *hear*? Remember your butterfly? Incidentally, there it is over there on that bush."

Peter quickly looks in the direction that Zachary is pointing, and sees it fluttering there, with its flickering wings radiating little rivulets of color as it moves about.

"Wait a minute, now, Zack. You promised you'd answer my questions, so don't disrupt that train of thought, okay?"

"Not at all. I wouldn't think of it. But didn't you learn more on Earth by doing than by simply hearing or observing?"

"Well, I guess so, but keep it simple, please, or else I'll lose this whole train of thought, and who knows when it'll come back so I can get these answers from you two."

"Very well," Zachary answers, "duly noted. Might I now ask you at this moment, Pete, to please stand?"

As Peter rises to his feet, Zachary and Paul do the same.

"Now, if you would, Pete, simply step over here in front of me, with Paul there behind you. Very good," as Peter positions himself. "Now then, remove my cloak that you're wearing."

Peter is looking directly into Zachary's eyes, questioning as he does.

"Stop now, Peter, before you ask the question, and think. Remember what we did before. Do you recall that?"

Peter, turning inward just a moment, recalls the activity. He remembers that he is first to will it to be so, and then to let it manifest. Zachary nods to Peter affirming that Peter has recalled the procedure correctly. Peter, noting Zachary's affirmation, closes his eyes a moment and wills himself to remove Zachary's cloak. A moment later, he opens his eyes, extends his hands in front of himself and grasps the cloak, pulling it off himself. Rather ceremoniously and deliberately, he folds it over his arm and extends it to Zachary.

Zachary reaches out, accepts the cloak and instantly it vanishes.

Peter has watched this in awe, noting that as the cloak disappeared, Zachary's appearance brightened brilliantly. "What was that? What happened to the cloak you gave me?"

Zachary smiles, "You asked me to keep it simple, Pete. That's as simple as I can make it for you."

Peter retorts jokingly, "Okay, Zack, I take back what I said about keeping it simple! Would you just go ahead and explain what happened?"

"Well, you already know the cloak I gave you is my own essence. When you gave it back, it became one with me again, resulting in the brilliant flash you perceived. Would you like me to give my cloak back to you? My 'loaner cloak?' Would you like it back?"

"Well, I would like to see how you actually produce it," replies Peter, "so that maybe I could do the same. So, would you pause at that point?"

"Alright," states Zachary.

Peter stares intensely to be certain that he won't miss one aspect of Zachary's actions. As he does, he perceives Zachary's eyes flicker for a moment, and then Zachary reaches around himself, cross-armed, and pulls. There, in his hands, is the loaner cloak.

"That's incredible, Zachary... absolutely incredible. I watched every motion, every moment when you did, and all I can tell you is, it's incredible. Can I do that? Can anyone here do that?"

Zachary smiles and, somewhat out of character for Zachary, answers seriously, "Anyone who has the will to do it, and is presented with a need to motivate that will, can indeed do so."

"You must show me how to do that!" exclaims Peter.

"Very well, Pete. Let me put this back on and I'll show you." With which, the cloak in Zachary's arms is slowly brought back, as though he were folding his arms onto himself, and instantly, it blends with Zachary's own raiment. "Very well. Now then follow these steps as I define them and demonstrate them to you. In just a moment, I will ask you to close your consciousness... close your eyes... shut down your external perception... go within. Understand that?"

"Got it. I know what you mean. I can do that."

"Okay, good. At that moment, think of yourself as the cloak. Don't think of yourself as a form – as Peter, or as anything – but think of yourself as your spirit, your energy, your being. Have you grasped that?"

"I think so, Zack. What you're saying is you want me to sort of focus on my sum and substance, or whatever it is that I am at this moment... you want me to focus on my 'being-ness'."

"Right! You've got it. Okay, now close your eyes and do just what you said."

Peter closes his eyes, and shuts down his external perception. As he does, he can still hear Zachary's voice, though it sounds strange and not at all the way he has become accustomed to hearing it, as if it's off in the distance.

"Good, Pete. Now, look for the center of your being. You'll know when you have reached that because you will feel the same kind of golden light that you saw in the friend you called 'Sir'."

Some brief time elapses, as Zachary observes Peter attempting to reach that point. Then Peter exclaims, "I have it. I've found the golden light."

"Good. Now, think it and then do it—first, create the need, structure the thought. Then focus your awareness and actualize it... make it real, give it substance."

Peter pauses for a prolonged moment and Zachary can see Peter's eyes flicker. Immediately, Zachary encourages him. "Good, Peter. Now, cross your arms in front of you and actualize what you have built with your thought."

Swiftly, without question, Peter mimics Zachary's earlier movements, and is startled to find that, as he reaches to hold it with each hand, he is actually grasping something of substance. But as he attempts to pull it to the front of him, as he saw Zachary do, he encounters substantial resistance.

"Don't let it bother you, Pete. Just continue. You've built the thought-form; you have the right to possess it. Continue on. It is your will. You're not fighting anything or anyone. It is your own will, and you have command over it. Produce your own cloak."

Peter continues, as Zachary has guided, though still noting some resistance, some strain.

Paul, speaking from behind Peter, states, "Peter, think of your butterfly. It is nothing different than that. Remember singing with Zachary? Well sing, Peter. Sing."

Peter recalls his efforts to sing. In that instance there is an almost audible pop. He opens his eyes and sees that, wondrously, there in his own hands is a golden garment, luminous with many colors, moving and pulsing. So startled is Peter, that he begins to snap and sparkle and crackle, and as he does, the cloak in his hands responds identically.

"Careful now, Pete," answers Zachary to an unspoken question. "Remember the purple flowers. Doubt caused them to disappear. Doubt is destructive to thought-forms. Faith is constructive to them. Got that?"

"Uh... yes. I... uh, understand that, but I don't know if I can keep it. I really don't."

"You can, Pete. It's your choice. If you don't want to keep it, that's fine. If you decide to keep it, understand that it's your choice, not mine, nor Paul's. One note I would add here. Remember the friend you call 'Sir'... he's counting on you... Wilbur needs our help. So, this is important, Peter. Give it all you've got."

Peter feels strangely inspired. The mere mention of the friend, the luminous one in the Hall of Wisdom, is sufficient to call forth a strange in-pouring of golden light, at which the cloak in his hands radiates this light and then settles down, and the colors become consistent and blend. Peter looks admiringly at this cloak, and turns to show it to Paul, his face beaming with accomplishment and joy.

Paul reflects this joy for Peter's accomplishment, nods placing his hands together, and gives Peter a gentle bow.

Peter turns back to Zachary with his golden cloak folded over his arm.

Zachary gives him an approving smile, nods, and seats himself. Then he looks up at Peter. "Well done, Pete... extremely well done. I don't believe I could have done better myself," and the intensity is broken with their joyous laughter. "Have a seat. Let's talk a bit more and see if you have any other potent questions rambling around in you."

Peter, still somewhat in a state of awe, slowly and almost mechanically turns and bends to seat himself, all the while holding in his outstretched arms this golden cloak, as though he were carrying a newborn child or something of a delicate and wondrous nature.

Zachary casts a quick glance at Paul, and they smile and nod at each other, pleased with Peter's accomplishments.

Peter states, "Zack, I must admit that whatever questions I had before, this experience has been so awesome that I can't remember a one. In this moment I am truly without words. I'm speechless. Except for this...

"With a hearty laugh, Zachary answers, "See? I knew he'd have a question. Didn't I tell you? He's always got a question."

Again, they share joyous laughter.

Finally Peter asks, "Well, my question is, quite simply... now that I've got it, what do I do with it?"

This so greatly humors Paul and Zachary that they are unable to contain themselves. Their laughter brings on the Realm of Joy around them again, and they find themselves rolling about, cascading in the light, the color, and the sound once more, all the while, Peter clinging to his golden cloak. Their laughter echoes off what seems to be distant walls and reverberates back to them, each time transformed into a new, joyous sound and collage of harmony. Colors swirl around them. After a while, they all lie down, stretched out in this sphere of wondrous color.

Peter rises up, perched on one elbow, and looks at his friends, "You know, fellows, I've told you this before, but I am so very fond of you. Never, ever can I recall feeling as wonderful as I do when the three of us are together like this, and particularly when we are in this state of... whatever... consciousness, or whatever it's called. It seems like we've always been together, and will always be together, and that we're actually a part of one another. It's almost magical. I just have to tell you again here how much I love and admire you both, and how thankful I am for your presence."

Both Zachary and Paul sit up and it is Paul who first speaks. "Peter, we know that, and we feel the same way. We thank you for expressing it. But might Zachary and I suggest this one concept for you to ponder.... do you think that the joy you have experienced here would be lessened if one of us, if Zachary or if I, were not here?"

Without a moment's hesitation, Peter responds, "You must be joking. After all, didn't you hear what I just said? I didn't say one of you. I meant both of you, totally and completely, of course. I would feel empty, in spite of the joy of the presence of one of you. I would feel like there's a hole, as though a great part of myself was missing. To be here, just two of us, either you or Zachary and I... well, I couldn't hardly bear the thought of not having you both present. Understand what I mean?"

"You have no idea how much we understand what you mean," responds Zachary. "Paul has granted me the privilege of telling you what I am about to say, and I thank him for that. Think about this, Peter... for a great span of time, while you were in the realm of Earth, it was Paul and I who visited this state of existence, this Realm of Joy... without *you*."

The instant the words are spoken, Peter realizes the true meaning of what Zachary is conveying. He realizes that his dearest friends, Paul and Zachary, feel the same way about him, and how much they must have longed for his presence before his arrival, his return. The inflowing of this realization, and the accompanying emotion, nearly overwhelms Peter. He starts to glow, and brilliant colors shoot forth from him, as his consciousness begins to grasp something far beyond his intellect, something which seems to reach all the way out into eternity – beyond time, beyond space, beyond the measure of a clock or a calendar – into infinity.

"You do understand, don't you, Peter?"

Barely capable of speaking, Peter stammers, "Oh, yes... I... I do understand, Zachary. Forgive me for not being with you and making this joy more complete, for it surely would be incomplete were one of us to be absent. In effect, when I was not here, I was depriving you of one-third of the quantity of joy. My deepest apologies. How could anyone ever withhold this wonder, this joy, from any other soul?"

The moment is electrified with Peter's awesome emotion. Yet Zachary and Paul do nothing to balance him. Though the colors come in great waves, swelling and cascading down over all of them, Zachary and Paul hold their positions, making no attempt to moderate Peter's emotion, as they have so oft done in past. Obviously, they intend that Peter should experience this, to know of it.

There follows the passage of much time, perhaps measured on Earth by the equivalent of weeks, months, or even years. It is a measurement which would for the most part be incomprehensible on Earth, for this experience is transpiring multi-dimensionally. It is not limited, nor measured in a straight line, but rather, all of Peter's existence is responding at once. Every single emotional event that Peter has ever experienced is now comparing this new insight and wisdom to the events that are a part of that experience. Each moment in any existence when he spoke out harshly because a loved one asked for a bit of his time and his attention, he recognizes that in that moment he had denied that entity this joy, the joy of union, of togetherness. Each time he had failed to answer a call for assistance, he now realizes that this was the joy that he had withheld from that call.

Peter's countenance turns from the brilliant hues of red, orange, green, yellow, and very swiftly becomes increasingly lavender, now a deeper purple, and now almost an incredibly rich, deep, blue-black indigo. Peter is aware of this, and is struck with a moment of fear. "What is happening? Zachary? Paul? What is happening? Where are we? Are we... dying?"

In that moment, Peter can feel, in the darkness, a familiar arm and hand fall upon each shoulder. Intuitively he knows to extend his own hands and arms, and they resume their triangular pattern. He can feel them spinning as a triangle through time and space, and in the moment of that greatest intensity, Peter becomes aware that he and Paul and Zachary are not three entities, but one.

He realizes that these three expressions, these three creations of God, were created intentionally to ultimately become one.

In the realization of this, an incredible brilliant white light appears, taking on golden hues—first as a small sphere, then growing, until a rivulet of light reaches out from its core and, focusing directly upon Peter, moves rhythmically but constantly towards him. Once it reaches him, it illuminates the trio, passing through and continuing on behind Peter, into time and space.

Looking into the faces of his friends, Peter answers his own question. "We were meant to be together, weren't we? Not together in the sense that we would lose our individual identities, but together in spirit... that we might come together for a greater good. Am I correct?"

Gently smiling, both Paul and Zachary nod.

"And there are others who are meant to be with us, as well," continues Peter. "Is that true?"

Still hovering in this ray of beautiful golden-white light, Zachary and Paul indicate their agreement with a smile.

"Now I understand what that entity meant. Wilbur is meant to be with us, isn't he?"

Both Paul and Zachary simply nod.

"And I have come to know and understand Wilbur better in all this, that I might help him to return to our group, as the two of you have helped me to return here. Is that true?"

For the first time since entering the light, Zachary speaks. "That is true, Peter. And there is much more… other discoveries to be made. But for now, unless Paul has another thought, I think your discovery is sufficient."

"I agree completely with Zachary," comments Paul. "I think it is time to get about our work. Zachary and I have much to do to assist you, but you must understand that it is now your work, if you so choose, to help Wilbur make similar discoveries as you have made. We shall help you, and be of support to you. That goes without saying. But it must be your doing, your choice.

"The reason for that is something which on Earth is called 'karma.' You have heard of it. We don't use the term here often, because it carries an implication of indebtedness, when in truth karma is a pathway of opportunity. The perspective of indebtedness is a concept peculiar to Earth. You don't owe Wilbur anything, nor does he owe you anything, but you have shared a common pathway that has left you both with the promise of opportunity."

At this point there is a pause, and both Zachary and Paul simply gaze upon Peter, waiting for him to absorb the meaning of what has been given.

Peter finally responds, "Well, what is the opportunity, if I might ask?"

"There are potentially many opportunities there, Peter. That would really be up to you to discern. But the point is, it would be better to assist Wilbur because you choose to do so, not out of a false sense of obligation or indebtedness."

Peter looks down, pondering that thought, and Paul and Zachary allow him these moments.

Finally, looking up again, Peter responds, "I choose to help Wilbur because I want to. I really like him, and I want to do all I can to help. Who knows, maybe I'll gain something, too," and Zachary and Paul smile lovingly at him, pleased at Peter's growing awakening.

Peter, the one who is directly facing the source of light, faces the light and states softly, "You know, from this position, looking into this wondrous light, it's the same as looking into the eyes of the entity in the Great Hall in our garden. Just the same," with which, Peter instantly realizes the source of the entity, his nature and his purpose.

Zachary speaks to the unspoken realization or thought within Peter, "That is a correct discovery, Peter. Retain it."

In that moment, the trio begins to slowly spin and rotate, tipping this way and that. Sound and colors begin to gradually appear and be heard, and the laughter begins again, and the trio once again moves into the Realm of Joy, of wondrous balance and ease. Peter becomes now balanced, as does Zachary and Paul.

After the passage of considerable time, the group awakens on the lush green expanse of the knoll in Peter's Garden Realm. Feeling remarkably rested and fit, Peter jumps to his feet, claps his hands together and rubs them and, looking at Zachary, states, "Well, how about giving a fellow a hand then, and let's get on with it."

Zachary jumps to his feet, and he and Peter extend their hands to lift Paul, as Zachary states, "Well, Pete, where is it? Where's Wilbur's realm?"

"Oh, right. Wilbur's realm."

"Care to lead?" asks Zachary of Peter.

"Not necessary, Zack. I like the way we've traveled in the past, and if you don't mind, I'd like to continue in the same manner."

Obviously pleased that Peter chose to have them initiate and perpetuate the movement, rather than explore it himself, Paul and Zachary each grasp one of Peter's arms, and they move swiftly down the knoll and into the luminous white mist As they do, it is Peter who breaks forth in song, followed by Zachary's laughter and swift imitation, and lastly by Paul.

As they emerge on the other side of the veil of luminosity, Peter hesitates for a moment as he observes the Crystal Workers' Realm now before them. Continuing down the path, Paul turns to Peter and asks, "How are you doing, Peter? Still feeling okay?"

"Yes, I am, Paul, and I thank you for your concern. I was just thinking, we'll have to show them, won't we? There's no reason why they can't have this realm look every bit as good and beautiful as ours, is there?"

"None whatsoever, Pete," answers Zack. "Just a bit of training in good gardening techniques. I'll be glad to handle that with you, if you'd like."

A ripple of laughter passes through our trio, and Peter responds, "Your assistance is most graciously accepted, Zack."

They approach the Crystal Workers' structure and, again, Peter can't help but notice the ornate, incredible workmanship of this structure. "How'd they manage that, anyway?" asks Peter. "I mean the appearance of this realm, the grounds and everything, is not the most orderly. At least, to my way of thinking, it certainly falls short of the perfection of our realm. Yet here is this incredibly crafted structure."

It is Paul who answers, "That's David's doing, Peter."

"David's doing?"

"Well, in a manner of speaking. Not his doing in the singular sense, but as the result of his efforts."

"I see. Is this a thought-form he's taught them?"

"Yes, in a manner of speaking," answers Paul again. "It is more of an attitude of expectancy. In other words, he's helped them to raise their level of expectancy. They don't comprehend it as a thought-form they themselves are building. Even though they know about thought-forms and constructing them, they haven't lifted their thought-forms to a potential beyond that of how they're using them to interact with Earth."

"Oh, I see. Listen, fellows, not to change the subject or anything, but since we're about to go in, could we take a bit of time first to discuss this and to figure out how we're going to help Wilbur?"

"Well, whatever you'd like, Pete," answers Zachary. "Remember what we told you. We'll support you in any way, of that you can be certain. But you must understand that first and foremost, there is the need to comply with what we've called in the past Universal Law, or free will choice. And since karma is involved here, it must be your doing."

They move over to a gentle slope off to the left of the structure. Peter looks back and forth as though he's hesitating to seat himself on the slope because it's a bit unkempt and disheveled.

"Not a problem, Pete," offers Zachary. "Just a moment." He pauses, steps in front of the other two, and in an instant this little spot, perhaps three to nine meters in height and width, is transformed into the perfection of Peter's Garden. Stepping back again, he turns to Peter and states, "Is that better?"

"Yes it is, thank you. Of course, you know what I'm going to ask you... didn't we... break a Law here, or do something wrong?"

"Well, let's sit down here and talk about it, and then, as you had asked, discuss what our approach might be with Wilbur. Is that acceptable?"

"Very well," states Peter, and the three of them seat themselves and begin their discussion.

Meanwhile, inside the structure, Wilbur is in his familiar corner. This time, however, he is looking about the room and then off into space, not at all focusing upon his work.

After a time, he rises and walks over to David, pausing respectfully, awaiting David's upward glance.

Responding to Wilbur's presence, David inquires,

"Welcome, Wilbur. How are you doing?" Rising to stand with Wilbur, he continues, "How may I help you, Wilbur?"

"I don't know, David. Things seem so different lately. I haven't been able to be as effective as I feel I have been in the past. It's as though something within me is changing. I can't seem to put the concentration, the energy, the effort, into my work. I do not wish, David, to create anything less than the very highest and best for my friends... those in need in the Earth. So I felt I must bring myself to you in this moment, David, recommending that you please relieve me, for a time at least, from my chosen duties, my chosen joys... as much as that saddens my heart." Wilbur looks down, as though he has failed and now must confront this failure in front of the one entity whom he respects most of all in this, the Crystal Workers' Realm.

With understanding, compassion, and a sense of gentle peace emanating from him, David steps forward and gently places an arm about Wilbur, continuing his stride and, with his arm embracing Wilbur, more or less pulling Wilbur along with him.

The two of them slowly walk forward as David continues to speak to Wilbur, and all the while they are striding directly towards the entrance to the great structure of the Crystal Workers' Realm, outside of which in this moment as we speak are reclined Peter, Paul, and Zachary.

If you were Peter, how would you communicate that which is unknown and has not yet been experienced to a 'Wilbur' who knows only the consciousness of his work and his one world? What would be your approach? How would you decide to share, as has been shared with you? How would you tell Wilbur of the wondrous joys awaiting him? And how would you accomplish this without imposing your beliefs, or getting in the way of that which he himself has chosen? In other words, how would you do all of this within the confines and the wondrous structure of free will and of Universal Law?

It will be good for you to question yourselves and to think on these things. For there will come a time when you will be called upon to do this very work.

CHAPTER 10

Sharing the Gift
DECEMBER 10, 1990

Peter is beginning to learn more about his own unlimited nature. Much of what he has gained through his recent experiences with Zachary and Paul, he will now share with Wilbur. In the process of that sharing, he will discover just how freeing those experiences have been for him.

Peter, Zachary, and Paul, have been discussing how to deal with the reawakening of their friend, Wilbur. They are reclined upon that expanse which has been, in essence, made pure or perfect by Zachary's actions.

"This is a nice bit of work, Zachary. I'd like to hear more about how you accomplished this, and of course I'd like to hear any thoughts you might have with regard to helping the crystal workers have this beauty throughout their realm. Is that possible... with us assisting of course? Is it?"

Zachary, stretched out, propped up on one elbow, glances up from the flowers he has been fussing with. "Yes, it is, Pete, and as long as all involved are willing, we can accomplish that as a joint work with them with comparative ease. It's not all that difficult. It primarily requires agreement on the part of all of them that this is something they would like to have. That agreement then enables us to function with them within the 'confines' of Universal Law."

"Zachary is correct, Peter," Paul joins in. "The essence of this involves the willingness of all of the souls involved. In this group-consciousness known as the Crystal

Workers' Realm, they as a group envision this realm as it is, just as you have on several occasions gone within yourself, envisioned or created a thought-form, and then came forth to make it manifest. That is a simplification of what is required to accomplish the objective about which you inquired. Do you understand?"

Peter, studying Paul, nods silently, for within him, he does understand.

After several moments of silence, it is Zachary who speaks again. "Peter, there are several things that Paul and I want to convey to you before Wilbur joins us."

Peter perks up and glances this way and that over Zachary's shoulder looking for Wilbur.

Before he can ask the question, Zachary continues on. "These are things which will help you and help us all to assist and be the best of service to Wilbur that we can... and to answer your question, yes, it is Wilbur who is going to join us, rather than we joining him." Smiling broadly as he states that, Zachary pauses only a moment and continues. "Do you recall, Peter, the several occasions that we have communicated without using speech? Do you remember that happening?"

Peter nods. "Yes."

"Well, then, remember that we can communicate in that same way. The three of us, and others if need be... we can facilitate a form of cooperative work, without tipping our hand to Wilbur."

"You see," adds Paul, "what Zachary means by 'tipping our hand' is to do something before Wilbur is ready to know about it. It is not in any way that we are trying to withhold something from him. It is simply that we are keeping lines of communication open between us and a greater consciousness, so that we can be of the best service to Wilbur in any moment of need. To a degree, it is even possible to suspend Wilbur's consciousness of time or movement while speech and actions take place, although that will probably not be necessary. However, if it should come to that, call upon us. Or call upon the consciousness required to enact such a... you might call it 'suspended animation' state. Nothing will seem abnormal to Wilbur or to us and nothing will actually stop. We will simply move perpendicularly to Wilbur's movement of time-consciousness, and then return with only the passage of, what you could consider to be, split-second time. Are you comprehending this?"

With his chin in his hand, Peter studies Paul and nods slightly, indicating he understands, but doesn't grasp it fully.

Zachary chuckles. "Look Pete, there's no need for one to grasp every nook and cranny of everything, you know. You just need to know of it and its essence, and know that you can employ that concept as you have a need. One doesn't need to be a clock-maker in order to tell time, after all."

They all chuckle a bit and the colored light descends and circulates around them, moderating the energy level somewhat. "By the way, Pete," continues Zachary, "you do know you still have that cloak over your shoulder, don't you? Remember?"

Startled, Peter glances over at his right shoulder and, sure enough, there is that golden fabric, emanating the light as his own cloak does, and with that, he realizes that he has come to Wilbur's realm in his own cloak and not Zachary's. Giggles come forth from Paul and Zachary as they are obviously observing his thoughts.

"Well, it seems as though I've accomplished something else, doesn't it, although the realization of that startles me just a bit, Zack. Somehow or other, I felt very comfortable, very secure, when I was wrapped in your cloak. Now here I am without it, and I'm feeling a bit naked I must tell you. But I guess, now that I think about it, I feel quite well and, interestingly, I feel a bit more perky, a bit more alert than I ever have before in Wilbur's realm."

It is Zachary who speaks again, though this time, very softly. "That is so good to hear, Pete. I'm thankful to hear it, and glad you have realized it. You are already complete, you see, and the less dependent you are upon things outside of yourself, the better off we'll all be. Not that there has been any loss by our sharing, not at all. To the contrary, whatever we give comes back to us many-fold over. And yes, Pete, we'll go into that later, too. But for now, it's a good realization. By the way, keep the cloak there on your shoulder. I have a hunch you'll find a use for it." Zachary tosses Peter a very broad, exaggerated wink, which causes both Paul and Peter to chuckle.

Peter is about to speak again, but Paul interrupts, "Well, Peter, unless you want to shift to another level of communication, we'll have to conclude this chat for a time, for if you'll look over there, here comes our friend Wilbur."

Swiftly turning, to the point that his swiftness almost rolls him over, Peter half turns, half stands, to look at the entrance. There, appearing in the doorway, he sees the glowing form of David, and at his side, Wilbur.

Finishing his movement by rising to his feet, Peter raises his arm to wave at David and Wilbur. As he does, he mentally notes that Wilbur's countenance looks less luminous than he has ever seen it. Indeed, it is in stark contrast to David's consistent glow, which he also notes appears more luminescent than he has ever recalled it. Comparatively, Wilbur looks puny. A wave of compassion sweeps over Peter, as though he is looking at a family member who is ill. He remembers the feeling, the sense of helplessness, and yet the stirring within of determination that he will contribute and that this dear one will get well.

With strong strides, Peter finds himself moving towards Wilbur with a surety and swiftness that startles even him. He can perceive a warm smile from David, and Wilbur expresses recognition of Peter, which Peter can tell by the increase in radiance in Wilbur's cloak. As he continues to move towards Wilbur and David, Peter detects the essence of a glow to his left and right and knows intuitively that there, at his sides, are Paul and Zachary.

Without a moment's hesitation, Wilbur steps forward and bows, a very large smile upon his face. "How nice to see you again, Peter, and you as well, Zachary, and indeed, Paul, you also. You are just what I needed today, just the answer to a prayer," at which they all smile at one another.

Peter comes forward and bows before David, and extends his hand to Wilbur. Wilbur casts a hesitant look at David, who nods an approval, and then Wilbur steps forward to grasp Peter's hand in his own. In that instant, a luminosity seems to move from Peter, as though one source of light or energy has infused another dimmer than itself, increasing the luminosity of the weaker.

"It is good to see you again, Wilbur. Paul and Zachary and I have been talking about you, and wanted to visit and see what you were up to. Are you well?"

With which, Wilbur falters a bit and looks down, then upwards at David again, whose tranquility reassures him. He looks back to Peter then and over his shoulder at Zachary and Paul, each to one side of Peter, and states, "Well, friends, I am honored, of course, that you should think to come and visit me. Your visit is timely. I had just told David here that I don't feel myself of late, and asked him if I might be temporarily relieved from my works."

Pausing awkwardly, as though he were admitting some wrongdoing, or revealing a flaw or fault in himself, Wilbur begins to stammer and to look away from Peter's eyes, which are radiating a wonderful warmth.

Peter searches for words with which to express himself. "Don't worry about it, Wilbur. We're glad you've been given some time off from your work. Why don't you come and join us over here on this little knoll. Our friend

Zachary here has done a splendid job of gardening."

Paul chuckles softly and the echo ripples through all five of them. Wilbur, rather nervously and awkwardly in his self-consciousness, dutifully follows the other four up the slight rise to Zachary's handiwork.

As the others seat themselves comfortably, Zachary casually sprawling himself out in his own inimitable style, Wilbur settles himself to a seated cross-legged position at the lower edge of the group.

"No, no, Wilbur, not down there. Up here with the rest of us," calls Peter.

"Are you sure, Peter?"

"Of course I'm sure. I'd be honored to have you right here alongside of me, if you'd like."

Wilbur adjusts himself as he sits between David and Peter. Off to the right, stretched out nearly prone, propped on an elbow, fingering some flowers is Zachary with a serene smile on his face. Paul, on the opposite side to the left, has seated himself upwards on the little mound and a bit off to the side but within an arm's length or so of Peter's back. Once everyone is comfortable, Peter turns to David. "David, we are honored to be with you again. This is indeed a blessing, to have you both with us. I do hope that this will not take you from any other important business."

Almost melodiously, David responds, "Not at all, Peter. My work is being cared for by others, and I am equally joyful and privileged to be here among you all."

David turns to Wilbur, who is more than just a bit awkward to be in the midst of these entities, all of whom he considers to be above his own stature. "Why don't you tell Peter what you have told me, Wilbur? Maybe he'll have some ideas or some insights for you," encourages David.

"Yes, please do, Wilbur, if it suits you," follows Peter.

"Well, I... uh... I wouldn't want to impose," stammers Wilbur.

"It wouldn't be imposing at all," replies Peter. "We welcome any thoughts about your experiences."

Somewhat reassured, Wilbur begins. "Well, you see, each day it seems as though something within me is changing. I can't quite express it to you, for it seems beyond expression. The energies with which I work are the same. They're pure, and they continue to flow just as always. The need on Earth is there, and so it's not a question of not answering a call.

"But somehow, deep within me, there's a growing incompleteness. I can't understand it. I have done all that I know to do to rectify and balance it. Yet, nothing seems to bring back the sense of purpose that I had before when doing these works with my friends and colleagues here in our realm. Does any of this make sense to you, Peter?"

"Perfectly. I understand all that you are saying."

Visibly reassured and pleased that Peter could grasp something which he, Wilbur, had felt to be, at the very best, vague, he is inspired and continues on. "I remember so many times, Peter, when there have been calls from the Earth. In those moments, I felt I was able to answer to the very best of the potential that was available for that call. But now it seems as though what I am doing, what I am bringing forth lacks something. It's as though I've lost something."

Pausing for a moment, Peter asks gently, "What do you think that is, Wilbur?"

Catching a wink from Zachary over on the side, Peter smiles inwardly and reflects that smile to Wilbur, who takes it as an encouragement.

"I don't know, Peter. I just can't seem to grasp it. It's as though all that I'm doing here is suddenly... well, insufficient. It's like I have been working here for so long." Pausing to reflect, "Why... I've forgotten how long. Do you remember how long it's been, David?" turning to speak to his trusted friend.

Looking down, David nods, "Yes, I remember, Wilbur. It has been quite some time."

Turning back to Peter, Wilbur continues. "It's not a thing, Peter, as much as it is a stirring within me. It's like there's something about to come forth from me. You know, like an idea that hasn't hatched, a thought that hasn't yet manifested. And I don't seem to have the energy or means to make it come into my focus of consciousness. So I just remain in a sort of limbo state... very uncomfortable for me. I have always been rather methodical and rather ordered, and have liked things to be somewhat structured. This throws me off balance. Do you understand what I am saying, Peter?"

"Yes, Wilbur, I do. That's the teacher in you coming out again, isn't it?"

Stammering just a bit, Wilbur gazes intently at Peter. "You... you know about that? I mean... you know about when I was a teacher?"

"Yes, I do. And a good one, as I recall."

Obviously impressed that Peter should know these details about him, Wilbur is reassured. His cloak begins to glow a bit more, though still very weak.

At that moment, Peter can hear inside of himself, *"Well, Pete, good time to give him a gift, don't you think?"*

Knowing where this is coming from, he glances at Zachary, who is still reclined, still fingering the flowers, and who gives him a wink.

Puzzled for a moment, as Peter tries to grasp what Zachary is conveying to him, he feels a tap on his shoulder. He turns to look at Paul, the source of the tap, and realization suddenly floods over him as he recognizes that his own personally made cloak is nicely folded and resting upon his shoulder.

With a quick questioning look at Zachary, *"Can I give this to Wilbur, Zack?"* he asks in his inner consciousness.

Zachary looks at him directly. *"Why not?"*

Peter and Zachary continue to gaze at one another for what seems to be prolonged moments. Wilbur is still looking down, fidgeting a bit, not aware of the communications that are taking place.

As Peter turns to glance at Wilbur, it is David's eyes that catch his. In that instant, he realizes that David, too, is aware of the communication between the trio, with which David smiles and nods, indicating his approval. Peter knows this is a confirmation, that this act would be a good one and would be acceptable.

Following an inner urging, Peter abruptly stands and reaches his hand down to his friend. "Wilbur, I think I know just what you need. You need a break. You need a bit of a change. And by the way, you look as though you're somewhat out of sorts."

Puzzled, Wilbur reaches up to grasp the outstretched hand of Peter and rises to his feet. "Well, thank you for your concern, Peter, but I have no wish to impose upon you in any way, nor my other friends here."

"No imposition, Wilbur. I have something here that perhaps you would like to use for a time. I believe it will make you feel better, and you can use it for as long as you'd like. When it no longer seems needed or desirable, you can simply return it."

"Why, thank you, Peter. What is it?"

With one swift motion that creates a luminous reaction, Peter sweeps the cloak down off his shoulder and approaches with outstretched hands, holding the cloak in front of Wilbur.

Wilbur's gaze falls upon the cloak. He is in obvious awe of it, for it radiates a golden luminosity he has only heretofore perceived on others who visited his realm. Looking quickly up into Peter's eyes, he asks, "For me, Peter? Do you mean it? I should wear this? I don't believe it would be appropriate." Then to his friend, "Would it, David?"

"Any gift lovingly given is appropriate, Wilbur," David warmly responds. "You know that from your own work. Peter wants you to have it. Therefore, shouldn't you accept it?"

Studying David carefully, Wilbur agrees, "Yes, that's true." Turning to Peter, he reaches his hands out to accept the cloak. As he does, his smile literally reaches to the core of Peter's being.

Golden rays of light bounce and ricochet within Peter's countenance, making him feel wondrously good. He can see Zachary and Paul responding as though they feel the same, as they glance knowingly at one another.

Zachary eyes the cloak lying across Wilbur's still outstretched arms. *"Well, Pete, better help him with it."* Suggests Zachary non-verbally, *"He doesn't know what to do next. Can you see that?"*

Looking back at Wilbur, who is standing somewhat dumbfounded, Peter steps forward. "Allow me, Wilbur." He grasps the cloak and swirls it about Wilbur in one swift motion and steps back to look at it. All the while, Wilbur is staring at Peter, more or less awestruck.

Peter steps back to Wilbur again, with self-assurance, and begins to brush and adjust the cloak as he does. "Looks good, Wilbur. I think it suits you, and fits you quite well. What do you think, fellows?"

"Looks great to me," answers Paul.

"Some of the best work I've ever seen," Zachary adds, chuckling a bit.

David simply nods and states softly, "It looks splendid, Wilbur. Splendid."

"Well, then, how do you feel, Wilbur?" asks Peter.

Wilbur's gaze shifts from the cloak and back to Peter, and back down to the cloak, "I feel great, just great. There's something about this cloak that seems to illuminate all aspects of my being. All of a sudden I feel secure, warm, very joyful, and the feeling of incompleteness seems to be fading away. What is this cloak, anyway, Peter?"

Remembering only too well his own questioning of Zachary when Zachary gave him a cloak, Peter somewhat mimics Zachary's comments, "Nothing at all, Wilbur. Just a little something I made for you."

Zachary rises to a seated position, and looks down, straightening and shifting his own cloak and then glances up to look at Peter, who returns his glance. It is obvious that both of them are amused at this replay of their earlier experiences together.

"Well, then," David offers, "now that you are so finely attired, Wilbur, it seems a shame not to go somewhere and do something, don't you think so, everyone?"

"A fine idea," adds Paul. What about you, Zachary? What would you say to all of us going somewhere?"

Zachary leaps to his feet with obvious enthusiasm, "You know me, Paul. Always ready for an outing, never the one to stay home. Always ready to go exploring and visiting. What do you say, Peter? Can we do it?"

Peter, a bit nervous at the attention and authority that is obviously focused upon him, looks into Wilbur's eyes as he answers, "It sounds like a good idea to me, but how about you, Wilbur? Would you care to take a little trip with us?"

Excitedly, Wilbur answers, "I would find that most enjoyable. Am I permitted, David?"

"Of course, Wilbur. You are in good company, and if it is something you think you would like, then you are welcome to go on the sojourn with our three friends here."

Wilbur looks quickly at David, as though he feels a bit of his security falling away as he realizes David won't be going along. He then sees Zachary standing there and smiles, "I suppose I couldn't be in better company. True, David?"

David smiles and nods. "No better company." With a wave, he turns to go back into the Crystal Workers' Hall.

Immediately, Peter reaches out to swiftly grasp one of Wilbur's arms, and Zachary grasps the other. Paul, then, steps forward in front, and off they go.

"Where would you like to go, Wilbur?" asks Paul over his shoulder.

Self-consciously, Wilbur states, "Well, uh... wherever you feel is appropriate. You fellows are certainly much more traveled than I, aren't you?"

With that, the three begin to laugh, which inspires Wilbur to join them in the laughter. As he does, he notices the wondrous lights and colors and a melodious sound coming, seemingly from beyond the group. He turns to Peter and asks, "Peter, what was that? Did you see that? Did you hear that?"

Receiving a knowing wink from Zachary as he leans over to glance at Peter, Peter states easily, "Yes, I did. Amazing, wasn't it? We'll have to explore that when we get to our destination."

Peter looks at Zachary, *"I guess I had a good teacher, didn't I, Zack?"*

"Well, Pete, that's counting unhatched chickens, isn't it? We'll see, won't we?"

Paul chuckles, and they return to verbal communication with Wilbur.

As they move along, Wilbur asks, "Could you tell me where we are going?"

"Of course," answers Peter. "It's a place we call the Garden Realm."

Paul takes this as the signal to lead the group into the misty veil of luminosity.

Wilbur is somewhat taken aback, hesitating. "Are you sure we can enter here, Peter? I've never done this before."

"Not a problem, Wilbur. We are capable, together as a group, of easily moving through this veil. And just to pass the time away, why don't we hum or sing a little?"

"Sing? You mean sing out loud? What will we sing?"

"Well, ask Zachary. He's one of the best at it."

Acting as though he were only just now hearing such a compliment, Zachary answers with feigned humility, "Oh, you don't mean it, Peter. My, such a compliment! I'm not all that good now."

"I have every confidence in you, Zack," Peter responds with humor. "Go on. Give us a tune. Start us off."

With which, Zachary swiftly raises his free arm and looking up at his up-stretched hand, followed by Wilbur's stare, there comes forth apparently from his hand the utterance of a most beautiful sound.

Struck with awe, Wilbur glances quickly over at Zachary to see where the sound is coming from. Noting that Zachary's mouth is not open, nor moving, Wilbur quickly turns back to Peter with a questioning look, and then smiles as Peter gives him a wink and a nod.

In a moment, the mist begins to separate and becomes less dense, and Wilbur sees that they are upon a pathway leading up to a small knoll resplendent with brilliant green, dotted with iridescent, brightly colored flowers. He notes that everything is marvelously, if not perfectly, kept, slowing down as he looks from this side to that at the radiance and the intensity of color. "Goodness me! This is beautiful. How wonderful to see such a place. Thank you all for bringing me here. What did you say this place is called?"

Paul answers, "We call it Peter's Garden, but you may call it the Garden, if it suits you."

"I like the sound of Peter's Garden rather than the Garden. It's more personal, you know. Just being here feels as though I'm surrounded by something that feels like Peter." He looks over at Peter, "Thank you, again, for bringing me here, and for loaning me this wondrous cloak. I'm feeling better every moment. I've never felt quite so calm and so strong, so wonderful. You know, at this point, I can hardly remember what it was that was bothering me before," with which, he himself begins to laugh, and they all echo Wilbur's laughter, the essence of it surrounding them once again.

"Peter, you must tell me, what is that? Each time we laugh, it's like the laughter creates color and light and music."

"Well, Wilbur, let's go over here while we talk about that. It's... uh... Zachary's favorite spot."

Zachary gives Peter a quick glance and grins, knowing that it is actually Peter's favorite spot.

Winking at Zachary, Peter points to the earth, and Zachary dutifully reclines himself in his normal fashion. Paul and Peter follow, and motion Wilbur to join them, forming a small circle, seated upon the lushness of the knoll.

Wilbur spends some moments looking around the wondrous expanse, as though he were drinking in the nourishment of the vivid color, the freshness and the resplendent energy present in all of the essences of this realm.

After some considerable time, it is Wilbur who is the first to speak. "You know, fellows, this place seems familiar to me, as though I have been here in a dream or something... as though a part of me has known this place. Does that make any sense?"

"It sure does," answers Peter.

"Yes, it does, Wilbur," adds Paul. "It makes a good deal of sense to all of us. By the way, we're glad that you are here, and that you are sharing your experiences with us. As we share, as you well know from your work with people in the Earth realm, and other realms, we each grow and gain so much. So, it is a privilege to be here with you, and to be sharing with you. Right, Zachary?"

"True, Paul. I couldn't have stated it better myself. Well done." Looking to Wilbur quickly, Zachary nods and winks exaggeratedly, which seems to settle Wilbur down.

Peter resumes, "Wilbur, I don't know about you, but somehow or other, I feel a need for a little rest. How about you, Zack?"

"You know me, Pete. Always ready for a little nap."

"Really?" questions Wilbur, as though he's never considered this. "Really, Peter? You mean, I could just lay back here and rest? It would be okay? No one would mind?"

"Not a bit. In fact, why don't you just stretch out here and relax, and we'll all join you."

Wilbur then leans back upon the wondrous earth. As he does, the lushness of the green grass seems to envelop him. The colors of the myriad of flowers beneath and around them infuse themselves into the energy, the envelopment around Wilbur, and in just a moment, Wilbur's eyes flicker and close. As they do, the cloak surrounding him shifts in its colors and begins to move in undulations of luminosity, indicating to our trio that Wilbur has gone into a state of spiritual rest.

Peter whispers, "Paul, shall we join him?"

"You needn't whisper, Peter, he can't hear you. No, I don't think so. Not this time. Let him have his rest and balance. He's going back into his consciousness and reviewing his spirituality, his records. And David is with him."

"What?" Peter exclaims.

"As I said, David is with him."

Looking here and there, Peter returns his gaze to Paul. "But, he didn't come with us. I saw him go inside the Crystal Workers' Hall."

"Stop a moment, Peter, and think," Zachary speaks up. "You're reacting. You're not thinking, you're intellectualizing. You're not drawing upon your wisdom. Remember. Remember what was told to you... that you had a helper in the Crystal Workers' Realm in the form of David."

Turning inward, Peter recalls the Golden One's comments, coming to a quick realization that David then must be capable of things beyond his own awareness at present and, perhaps, to a very great degree, things beyond his own experiences.

"So are you saying, Paul," queries Peter, "that David has joined him, more or less in a spiritual form?"

"Basically, yes... the essence might indeed be called spiritual. But it is also very much a level of existence, definable and identifiable, see?"

"Okay. Well, I think I've got that. So then, what do we do next?"

"Well, what do you think?" asks Zachary. "What do you feel should be done next?"

A bit puzzled, Peter looks down at Wilbur, surrounded by the rhythmic movement of light, and then decides to go within himself once again. He begins to hear a consciousness, in a sense... as though knowledge is coming to him. Not spoken or communicated in the normal means that he is accustomed to; rather, it is realized within him, as though he is discovering it in great large chunks. Within these discoveries, he recognizes that Wilbur will be much more balanced when he awakens. He also knows that he will be able to tell when Wilbur shall awaken by observing Wilbur's outer countenance.

"Well done," he hears within his consciousness, recognizing the words to be Zachary's.

Peter opens his eyes and re-awakens his senses, and looks into the eyes of Zachary.

"Very good, Peter," comments Paul. "Good deduction. Take a look at Wilbur now. What do you see?"

As he observes Wilbur, Peter notes that the movement of the colors and the luminosity has begun to change, and there is a golden glow once again coming from within Wilbur, growing and blending with all the other colors, and then notes that Wilbur's eyes begin to flicker.

Wilbur's eyes open, and he looks up at Peter, at first a bit startled. Then obviously recalling where he is and who he's with, he sits up, rubbing his eyes, slightly embarrassed, "Gosh, have I been gone long? I hope I haven't kept you."

"Not at all," answers Peter, turning away to hide his amusement, as he recalls having himself said the very same words numerous times to Paul and Zachary. "Not to worry. We have had a good rest ourselves, haven't we, fellows?"

"Oh, yes, indeed," responds Zachary, and Paul nods. Zachary continues on, "You know me. I can rest at the drop of a hat. By the way, I wish I had a hat. I miss those. They always give one the appearance of some status. You know what I mean, Pete?"

Chuckling just a bit, Peter responds, "Not exactly, Zachary. Perhaps you'd care to explain," leading him on.

"Well, as I said," rising to his feet, "I like hats. I've always had a thing about them. Paul will tell you."

Smiling broadly, Paul nods, looks down and begins fidgeting with the grass so as not to reveal his humor at what he knows is about to take place.

Wilbur turns from one to the other, uncertain of what is to transpire.

As Zachary strides to the front of the group, Peter asks, knowing what is coming next, "Well, Zack, what will it be? A Stetson? A derby? Perhaps a wizard's cap?"

"Ah, yes... a wizard's cap! I like those. Let's see now..." Looking down and closing his eyes for a moment, Zachary swiftly raises his right arm up into the air, swirls his forefinger rapidly, and opens his palm. There is a melodious sound and a burst of color as a brilliant blue conical-shaped hat appears, spinning around on his hand, decorated with golden crescents and symbols of all shapes and sizes. Dangling from the top is a tassel woven out of dazzling golden fibers that appear to be sheer light. As Zachary continues to spin the conical hat on his hand, still upraised, the tassel sprays little rivulets of golden light everywhere.

Looking up as though in amazement himself, Zachary studies his creation. "Well it's a bit flashy, but quite fitting. What you think, fellows? Does it suit me?" and in a single motion he brings it down and places it firmly on his head, turning this way and that to demonstrate it to his friends.

It is Peter who first begins to laugh uproariously, rolling about, followed by Paul whose laughter can be heard firm and strong well above Peter's. Finally Wilbur, apprehensively looking from one to the other, joins in, as Zachary strides animatedly back and forth, assuming different poses as though he were, indeed, some sort of wizard.

Then with a swift motion, Zachary removes the hat and more or less throws himself down onto the ground with the other three and laughs with them. As the light and sound and color spill over all of them from their laughter, Wilbur is caught up in this new experience of the free expression of joy.

After awhile, when their laughter subsides, they all look at one another and place their arms upon each other's shoulders, as though in sharing this moment of sheer joy, they want to confirm it by touching.

Peter comments, as they embrace, "Well, we haven't had a good laugh like that for a long time... too long, in fact. How about you, Wilbur?"

"Oh my! Seems like an eternity or two. That's the best laugh I've had since I can remember. But Zachary... how did you create that hat? Do you think I could ever do that?"

Chuckling, Zachary looks down at the hat now resting on its side next to him and states, "Goodness. These questions remind me of an old friend of mine. Must be some sort of contagious affliction." Peter begins to laugh again, then Paul, then Wilbur, and the four of them start all over again.

Finally, Peter turns to Wilbur. "You know, Wilbur, we also saw and heard and felt what you experienced. It's wonderful, isn't it? It comes from a source which is unlimited. Some would call it the Realm of Joy. Some might call it the Realm of Laughter. But whatever you would call it, it is very healing, very joyful, and it's such a blessing when it's shared. We're very glad that it has pleased you."

"Yes, indeed," adds Paul.

"No question about it," echoes Zachary.

"Well, I don't understand it," comments Wilbur. "Never have I seen anything like it. But I wouldn't have missed it for anything."

"Well then, would you like to know more about hat creating?" asks Zachary.

"Oh, yes, I would, Zack."

"Well, I don't know. Paul? Do you think he's ready?"

"Oh, I do indeed, Zachary."

"And, Peter... do you think I am capable of teaching Wilbur? He's been a teacher himself, you know. Goodness, he might be critiquing every move and action I make."

Embarrassed, Wilbur begins to stammer and speak, "Oh... oh, no... not at all."

It is Peter who reaches out to touch Wilbur on his shoulder. "Not to concern, Wilbur. That's just Zachary's way. He's having a bit of fun with us. He'll go ahead and teach you, no matter what you say. Right, Zack?"

"Well, a guy's got to bear in mind who he's working for and what his duties are, don't you see? And if I'm to teach hat-making, never let it be said that Zachary would do less than his best."

Without another word, Zachary rises to his feet, reaching a hand down to Wilbur, who readily grasps it. As Zachary pulls him to an upright position, he looks into his eyes. "Now the first thing here, Wilbur, is to let go of your own limitations."

"Limitations?"

"Yep. Limitations."

Puzzling for a moment, Wilbur looks over his shoulder at Peter.

Peter nods, "Go ahead. Just try to follow what Zachary's telling you."

Zachary tells Wilbur to close his eyes, shut down his

sensory perception, and to find the center of his being. Wilbur does so, and after a few moments, he hears Zachary say, "Now, think of a hat."

"What kind of a hat?" asks Wilbur.

"Any hat. Whichever hat suits you."

"Well, I've always wanted a bowler. Do you know what that is?"

"Doesn't matter whether I know of it," answers Zachary, all the while Wilbur's eyes are closed. "It's important that you know of it."

"Okay," answers Wilbur dutifully. "What do I do next?"

"First, you image it. You think about it. You manifest it in your mind. First, bring about the intent. You have to create the pattern, the blueprint. Tell me when you've got it firmly."

Concentrating, Wilbur images a splendid bowler in his mind. As he does, he hears Zachary say, "Excellent. Now, open your eyes and manifest it."

Opening his eyes, Wilbur looks questioningly at Zachary, who stands immediately before him, looking directly and steadily into Wilbur's eyes.

Wilbur asks weakly, "How... how do I do that, Zachary?"

"Just do what I did," answers Zachary encouragingly and with deliberateness. "Do exactly what I did."

Blinking his eyes a few times in recollection of the image, Wilbur raises his hand upright and swirls his fingertip up into the air. Instantly, there is a melodious sound. Color and light swirl downwards, and there, rotating on a fingertip, is a beautiful new bowler hat.

Astounded, Wilbur drops the hat.

"Allow me, Wilbur. Please," and Zachary reaches down to pick the bowler up from the ground, brushes it off and hands it to Wilbur. "Nicely done, a grand hat. Wouldn't be my choice, of course – a bit too bland for my taste – but lovely, nonetheless.

Still awestruck, Wilbur looks at the hat, turning it around and around in his hand. Doubt begins to creep into his consciousness, and he now looks to Peter, "This is impossible. I couldn't have created this." As he does, the hat feels as though it were alive, tingling.

Immediately, Zachary states, "Careful there now, Wilbur. One needs faith. Remember? Remember your work. Doubt dissipates, faith concentrates. Remember?"

"Oh, yes. Sorry," at which time he draws himself inwardly in a manner which even Peter finds amazing to witness. Instead of sparkling and snapping and cracking as Peter knew himself to do from time to time, Wilbur's outer countenance simply swirls with radiant swatches of color, draped this way and that over him. It is as though he is being bathed in a collage of color. "I have it now! I have it strong."

"Well then, plop it on your head and we'd best be off. I know that David is wondering about us, and perhaps we should get back."

Before Wilbur can respond, Peter and Zachary each grasp one of his arms, Paul resumes the lead, and off they go. Zachary commences a song, as he thrusts his hand upward, imitating a drum major, and begins marching as though he were leading a parade. They all follow his lead and bounce along as they fall into a sort of haphazard cadence. In a moment they pass into and through the veil of luminosity and swiftly find themselves walking along the pathway towards the Crystal Workers' Hall.

Once they reach the beautiful little knoll that Zachary had gardened, Peter suggests that Wilbur seat himself, and the others do the same.

Almost immediately, David can be seen emerging from the hall, striding up to them. "Hello, everyone, did you have a good outing?"

Wilbur excitedly rises to his knees to tell of their adventures.

Smiling, David takes a position with the group.

In a lull in Wilbur's animated recounting, Peter suggests, "All this traveling has made me weary again. How about you Wilbur? How about a brief rest, and we'll come back to this, if David would permit, after we've all had a chance to re-balance ourselves. What do you say, fellows?"

"Well, I think it's a good idea," replies Wilbur. "I'm not sure it's what I want, but I know that you are wise, Peter, and so I accept your suggestion."

With this, they talk quietly for a bit and ultimately Wilbur drifts off into a state of rest and balance, followed closely by David. Just a bit further behind is Peter.

―――――――――――

We ask of each of you to be mindful that Wilbur's experiences are not unlike those of your own. Whether you believe or disbelieve something, is dependent upon your willingness to trust.

Illuminate the aspect of trust within you in this time and that which lies ahead. For trust is a key, an important one, associated with faith. It is that which can very strongly build a creative force beyond your belief.

CHAPTER 11

Ceremony of the Crystals

DECEMBER 11, 1990

In profound thankfulness for the opportunity to have been with you in this journey, following Peter and his friends, we would now like to share with you the joy and radiance of a most wondrous ceremony.

This then is our humble offering of blessing. We share it with you as our gift to all of you there in the realm of Earth.

May it prevail in your hearts and spirits forever.

The group is sitting on the grass before the entrance of the Crystal Workers' Hall. They have stirred to re-awakening and have discussed to great length their experiences, joyfully and with wonder, and much has been revealed to Wilbur, whose knowledge and acceptance have grown remarkably. A great deal of what Wilbur has experienced in the time which has passed has paralleled to a remarkable degree the experiences that Peter had shared with Zachary and Paul.

David is speaking softly, "Wilbur, perhaps it would be good to invite our friends to the great festivities about to take place. If you are willing and it would be your choice to do so, we would be pleased to have them."

Pausing only for a moment, Wilbur takes on a radiance as he comes to an understanding of what David is suggesting. He turns to face Peter, Zachary, and Paul, "My dear friends, I am so grateful and joyful for having had the honor to share with you as we have, and Peter, there is no question that I am unworthy of the radiant cloak you have given me, from which I am benefiting so greatly. I feel renewed beyond anything I have ever imagined possible."

Peter looks down, somewhat embarrassed, "It is my honor." Glancing at Paul and Zachary then back to Wilbur, "It is a privilege for all of us, Wilbur, for what you are wearing is not only from me, but from us all, here and beyond."

Nodding an affirmation of understanding, Wilbur continues, "David has invited me to ask all of you to join with us in the great ceremonies as are about to take place. Some of these will take place in our realm, as I'm sure there will be others in your own."

Puzzled by what is being spoken, Peter turns to look at Zachary and Paul, and receives a warm knowing nod from Paul and a grand wink from Zachary. From this Peter knows there is something here that they will later explain to him.

Looking directly at Peter, Wilbur asks, "Would you, then, honor us by joining our ceremonies?"

Without a hesitation, Peter feels and hears within himself the affirmation from both Paul and Zachary, and responds, "We would be honored. We'll follow as you lead."

Rising immediately, David leads the way, followed by Wilbur, and the trio. As they enter the hall of the crystal workers, Peter notes immediately a radiance within the structure that he had not seen previously. There seems to be a luminosity reaching fingers of light from beneath the hall and off to the side. Opposite the tables of the crystal workers, the entirety of the wall has opened to reveal a broad expanse of a deep indigo sky, as might be seen from the Earth on a moonless night. The stars are abundant, and occasionally rays or groups of cloud-like color move very subtly across the sky.

Looking to the opposite side of the room, Peter notes that there are many entities here now, and that their cloaks are luminous, much moreso than he has ever seen in past. Puzzled, yet following along rather dutifully, he looks back over his shoulder to Zachary, and receives a wink.

It is David now who comes to a stop and motions to the others to seat themselves before a great long table, perfectly though simply crafted of some sort of stone or mineral substance. It cannot compare to the table in the Great Hall, but is nonetheless some artisan's wondrous labor of love.

As they seat themselves, David moves to the opposite side of the table, framed by the open expanse of rich, deep indigo behind him, dotted with rays of light, flickering and sparkling as a crown decked with star-like jewels.

He turns to face the crystal workers, as well as Peter's group now seated at the table, and Peter is awed as he notes that David begins gradually but very evidentially to take on a glowing, golden radiance. It is as though he has been transposed by another entity, and yet David's personality and consciousness are ever-present while merging with this additional countenance.

In a moment, rays of golden white light reach out as though anointing or blessing each member present in the great room of the Crystal Workers' Hall. All feel the impact.

Peter looks from side to side and notes that there are exquisitely crafted crystals standing here and there. Each is now giving off a tonal radiance, blending into a wondrous masterpiece of ever-increasing light and melodious sound, as one by one, crystal workers bring their own individual work, to be placed side by side—each uniquely different, each giving off a different hue, a different tone.

Finally, when all have brought their gifts forward, David raises his arms in a motion not unlike that which Peter has so often seen his friend Zachary do. As he does, there is a wondrous expansion of sound and light. The colors race around the room as though they are a myriad of spotlights, shining here and there, sending rivulets of light off the prismatic faces of each crystal.

The sound moves to a crescendo, far beyond anything Peter can recall ever hearing before. The music then blends into a symphonic resonance, which transcends Peter's very being. Turning to look at Zachary, and Paul, and Wilbur, he can see the radiance pouring from each of them as well, as they turn to smile back at him.

Looking over his shoulder and about the room, he meets the warm glance returned to him from entity after entity, obviously crystal workers, and perhaps others who have come here for this, the Ceremony of the Crystals.

David turns then to face the darkness, the resplendent, incredibly rich indigo color. And as he does so, fingers of light race to and from the crystals, back and forth, reaching out into the darkness. They seem to reach some unseen distant destination, and there is a resonance as though an echo could be heard in some Earthly canyon; but here, in this celestial canyon of existence, the echo reverberates at the core of Peter's being, the inner chamber of his own golden light.

It seems to Peter as though his light is struggling to come forth. He fights to contain it, fearing that he may be on the verge of one of his sparkling, crackling episodes, which might disrupt this incredible ceremony, feeling the intensity of the struggle growing within him.

Looking quickly to Paul and then to Zachary, he sees from Paul an understanding, and receives a look from Zachary as though to say, *Don't fight it. Just be.*

Knowing, or feeling, that assurance from Zachary, Peter gradually releases, and the golden feeling comes forth from within him, spilling out into the room. There is the sound of muffled voices as others observe Peter's golden light. David steps off to the side, allowing the light radiating from Peter to reach forth.

Now unobstructed, Peter's golden light races forward, striking the crystals, one by one. They in turn reciprocate with a rainbow-like cascade of color back to Peter, emanating off him to the sides, right and left, and behind him. And as it does, Peter can see Zachary responding in just the same way.

Colors race from Zachary and are reflected from the crystals. Then from Paul come blue-whites and beautiful pastel reds, and from Wilbur flow all sorts of greens, golds, and yellows; and then from the next, and behind, and over to the right, and to the left—all present, in succession, open and allow the inner core of their own light to enjoin with the light of each of the others in this great Crystal Workers' Realm.

Even the crystals themselves seem to be a part of all of this, vibrating and glowing fingers of light racing out from them… to the Earth, and as though being responded to from Earth, the light returns to them, echoing and reverberating in the room.

Peter is filled with awe and wonder as this continues for an unknown period of time. Finally, the color begins to subside and the sound grows to what Peter interprets as a wondrous choral, harmonious sound. Without being capable of discerning a melody, Peter knows there is one. It flows and undulates, filling the room with wonder, as the light now remains consistent in a golden-white hue.

In time, the light seems to move inward, each entity absorbing a quantity of this, including Peter, and then the room returns to a sense of normalcy. Only the crystals themselves are effervescing a glow of a collage of color, light, and sound, ever so softly as though to support, as an ensemble, the choral music coming from unseen realms.

In that moment, the awesome depth of the vista in front of Peter calls his attention. Transfixed, he begins to see a great glowing orb of brilliant white light moving slowly from what he assesses to be behind or above them. It is heading out into the distance and depth of the indigo, the deep jet blue-black, as though an immeasurably deep fabric of velvet were stretched out before them, continuing to move obviously towards a distant point until it can no longer be seen.

After a time, there is another sphere that moves outward, gently, in a rippling undulating motion until it too seems to indicate that it has reached its destination. And then another moves towards this distant point, and another, and another.

Peter turns to Zachary, who indicates it is acceptable for him to speak in their inner consciousness. Without words, Peter asks, *This is wondrous. What is it? What is happening?*

Peter, this is what you know on Earth as Christmas.

Stunned for a moment, Peter cannot find words with which to express a flood of memories—a vision of his family, their tree, their home gaily bedecked, the presents, the Christmas dinner, the friends. It all passes before him. Following this, each year of his life echoes, on and on, until he has reached his own childhood. Then he sees a baby. Then darkness, and then he perceives a great orb of brilliant white light as it begins to move away from the Earth and up and up into an indigo eternity.

Peter turns to Zachary, who nods and winks ever so slightly.

Zachary, continues Peter non-verbally, *I just saw my entire life... at least the portions that were Christmastimes, each one, one right after the other, and then I saw a baby... me, I guess. After that, I saw one of those lights... as you see them now, out there, going down. Are they going to the Earth?*

Yes, answers Zachary.

Are they children? Are they babies?

No.

Then what are they? That's what I saw after I saw the baby.

They are blessings. They are, what you would call, the answer to prayers, Peter.

Turning inward, Peter reflects. Coming to a realization, he turns to Zachary again with the thought, *Was I the answer to a prayer? Is that why I saw one of these lights after I saw myself as a baby?*

Yes, Zachary smiles to Peter. *You were, indeed, the answer to prayer... your parents' prayers.*

Almost overwhelmed with joy and emotion, Peter turns intensely within himself. As he does, he feels the familiar touch to his right and left from Paul and Zachary.

He hears from Zachary, *Not a problem, Peter. Go ahead and experience those memories. We are right here beside you. There is nothing to concern over.*

Relieved, Peter goes even deeper within himself. Emotion begins to pound him. First this color and that, then the overwhelming memory of his dear wife, Stephanie, his children, his grandchildren, his friends. And Abe.

And Abe... where is Abe? he wonders almost aloud.

Zachary continues his gentle encouragement, *Take a look. Remember, we're with you. Go ahead and look for Abe.*

Just how do I do that?

It is Paul who answers now, *In spirit, in higher consciousness, by knowing your intent... just the way you created a butterfly, the way Wilbur created a hat. First, create the desire, and then allow it to manifest before you.*

Remembering the process, Peter closes his eyes and envisions his friend Abe. Somewhere deep within him, a pang of loneliness, of familiarity, tugs at his being, and he sees every wrinkle on dear Abe's face. He sees the small cap on Abe's head, the one he often joked good-naturedly about with his Jewish friend.

Now create, he hears from Paul.

Mustering his concentration, Peter now brings himself back to full consciousness, opens his eyes, and to his wonder, there before him, as though upon a dark screen, is projected the presence of Abe and Abe's family.

It is Hanukkah, and they are at the evening ceremony and meal. The candles are lit. They have sung their first song, and have all come together to exchange blessings and a gift.

It is Abe who speaks, and Peter clearly hears his

friend's voice. "If you would, my family, join with me in prayer, as I remember my dear friend, Peter, who has gone on before us."

As Peter continues to hear Abe speak of him and ask his family for prayers for him, he can see spheres of light heading towards him. In a moment of concern, he hastily looks to Zachary and then to Paul, whose grasp of his shoulders remains firm.

Not a problem, Peter. Don't worry. Just be still, and open to it.

Turning back to observe the small spheres of light moving swiftly towards him, Peter feels the instance each sphere strikes his being, which fills him with a feeling of immense joy and love. He is radiant with the brilliance of these bluish-white spheres of light—the prayers of Abe and his family.

As he hears Abe utter the words to conclude the prayer ceremony, the window closes. The vision passes. But Peter remains luminous in the blue-white glow of the prayers, which have been spoken in his name.

And my family? Are they well?

See for yourself, responds Paul.

Immediately, as though now automatic for Peter, he closes himself and visualizes, first his wife and then his children. Then, opening his eyes he sees before himself their grand dining-room table. At the head of it, a chair is empty, but there is joy in the faces of all present. His wife calls for all to join together, to join hands across and around the table, as was their custom.

Again, the lights come to Peter. This time, he accepts them warmly and openly, becoming resplendent in their presence. The instant that they are complete, Peter moves within himself and asks with fondness, *Zachary, Paul, will you join me in prayer for my family, for my friend Abe, his family, and my friends?*

Each responds affirmatively, and Peter can see great spheres of undulating light hurtling from them off into the distance, into the vastness of the indigo, one after another, and another, and another.

Peter then becomes aware that the spheres are coming not only from himself and Paul and Zachary, but Wilbur too has joined in, and David, and all of the crystal workers. They have entwined their arms upon one another's shoulders and have gathered to face the great velvety darkness. The spheres, trailing streams of light, become so frequent and numerous that they are as fingers of light reaching towards Peter's family, and into the depths of eternity.

In that moment, again, a wondrous sound can be heard, as though all of the heavenly host were rejoicing. After the stream of prayers begins to subside, the remaining energy, the joy, the emotion is near to overwhelming. Then there appears a beautiful light. First, it is only a small spot growing, with rays extending from it, dancing, flickering, as though the core of it were of such immeasurable intensity that it is an effort unto itself to contain its very radiance.

In the moments that follow, Peter loses his consciousness, though remaining aware of the presence of each one: of Paul, Zachary, Wilbur, David, and others, as he feels himself hurtling into the light.

Finally, at the central core of what Peter experiences as the most intense light he could ever imagine, he finds, within it, a sense of well-being, a sense of eternity; and in his heart and mind, there is a knowing. It is a knowing that each prayer for those for whom he has prayed has been heard and answered, and that each of these loved souls will one time, one day, return to be together.

Within the light, Peter looks and sees his parents, who had gone on before, smiling and waving to him, blowing him kisses. There, too, are his grandparents, and a dear aunt, and other friends, all in the presence of this wondrous light. The wonder is so great that he knows not of himself, but only of the Oneness of all beings. He can find naught but joy. In the familiar faces of his family and friends who had preceded him in departing the Earth, he can see only a sense of love and compassion, and a sense of peace.

Peter cannot measure any time or space or distance, and knows not how long he has dwelled in this consciousness. It is only by the gentle touching of his friends, Paul and Zachary, that he first begins to stir back to his own consciousness. As he does so, he is amazed to find himself upon his beloved knoll back in his Garden, looking across the resplendent colors, the wondrously manicured landscape, the bright-colored hues of the flowers, the trees, the bushes...

Looking around, he sees that, aside from Paul and Zachary, no one else is present. "Goodness, I hope I didn't embarrass you. I lost control of it there, such wondrous things happened. I couldn't begin to tell you, but then I presume you know it, for I am certain you were with me."

Looking down at Peter who is still reclined, Paul states only, "Merry Christmas, Peter."

"Yes, Peter, Merry Christmas," adds Zachary, "and Happy Hanukkah, too."

May the spirit of this Christ Mass live on within you throughout eternity, and may this, our humble gift of your participation in Peter's first Christmas in these realms, be a light and an inspiration for the remainder of your duration in the realm of Earth.

In times which lie ahead, we ask that you remember that, as God is expressed into consciousness, so are you expressed as eternal and unlimited creations of God. You are His living expressions. You cannot be lost nor altered, for you are unique, and in that uniqueness does God find eternal beauty. As each flower afield, He knows you, everyone.

We pray that this work as has been given herein, and those which follow in the continuation of Peter's journey, might promote an understanding with which you can meet and manage each event or circumstance during your sojourn there on Earth.

We pray, further, that these shall thus make the way that much moreso passable for you, as you move beyond this incarnation and into realms beyond.

–Lama Sing

A Note from Al and Susan Miner...

The complete works of the Peter Project include more than 200 readings, and take place over a period of 10 years.

The Project includes two components:
- The Peter Chronicles.
- Questions about the chronicles submitted to Lama Sing by members participating in the project at that time.

Many people feel that the greatest wealth of information lies in the Q&A readings, which actually make up more than two-thirds of the Peter Project.

We are very pleased that these Q&A readings are being made available as companion books, a tool for further understanding, to each of the Chronicle books.

Books by Al Miner & Lama Sing

The Chosen: *Back Story to the Essene Legacy*
The Promise: *Book I of The Essene Legacy*
The Awakening: *Book II of The Essene Legacy*
The Path: *Book III of The Essene Legacy*

In Realms Beyond: *Book I of The Peter Chronicles*
In Realms Beyond: *Study Guide*
Awakening Hope: *Book II of The Peter Chronicles*

How to Prepare for The Journey:
     Vol I Death, Dying, and Beyond
     Vol II *The Sea of Faces*

Jesus: *Book I*
Jesus: *Book II*

The Course in Mastery

When Comes the Call

Seed Thoughts
Seed Thoughts to Consciousness

For a comprehensive list of readings transcripts available, visit the Lama Sing library at www.lamasing.net

About Al Miner

A chance hypnosis session in 1973 began Al's tenure as the channel for Lama Sing. Since then, nearly 10,000 readings have been given in a trance state answering technical and personal questions on such topics as science, health and disease, history, geophysics, spirituality, philosophy, metaphysics, past and future times, and much more. The validity of the information has been substantiated and documented by research institutions and individuals. Those receiving personal readings continue to refer others to Al's work based on the accuracy and integrity of the information in their readings. In 1984, St. Johns University awarded Al an honorary doctoral degree in parapsychology.

Al conducts a variety of field research projects, as well as occasional workshops and lectures. He occasionally accepts requests for personal readings, but is mostly devoting his remaining time to works intended to be good for all. Much of his current research is dedicated to the concept that the best of all guidance is that which comes from within.

Al lives with his family in the mountains of Western North Carolina.